Women

in

King Philip's War

Women

in

King Philip's War

compiled and edited

by

Edward Lodi

ROCK VILLAGE
PUBLISHING

Middleborough, Massachusetts

ISBN 978-1-934400-25-8

Rock Village Publishing
41 Walnut Street
Middleborough MA 02346

(508) 946-4738

rockvillage@verizon.net

Dedication

To Yolanda, who conceived the idea for this book

Contents

Preface 3

Time Line 7

The Squaw Sachems 19

    Awashonks 21

    Weetamoo 39

    Quaiapen (the Old Queen) 49

Mary Rowlandson 57

Harpies, Housewives, and Heroines 95

    The Heroic Girl at the Door 99

    Stratagem and Stealth 101

    Escape by Needle and Thread 105

    Signal by Pounding 109

    Hurrah for Hannah! 111

    The Gentler Sex? 113

    The Milk of Human Kindness 115

    Penelope Winslow 117

    Wootonekanuske 129

    Amie 135

    No Pew of Their Own 137

Give Us This Day Our Daily Dread 139

Appendix I: Political Correctness............................145

Appendix II: Fireside Industries 147

Appendix III: The Queen's Fort............................157

Recommended Reading..161

Bibliography..163

Women

in

King Philip's War

Preface

This book came about as a result of a talk I gave at a monthly meeting of the Sippican Women's Club in Marion, Massachusetts. The club official who asked me to give the talk knew that I had written several books about King Philip's War, and thought that the subject might be of interest to her fellow members. I, however, at first had misgivings. The bloodiest war ever fought in New England (and, in terms of the percentage of the population killed, the bloodiest ever fought on American soil) a suitable topic for a group of women?

Nowadays of course women play an active role in the military, but even so, war as a topic generally attracts far more men than it does women. The women of Sippican, at their regularly scheduled meeting, would be a captive audience. Would they be bored, or worse, repelled by what I had to say?

But what if I tailored the talk to their specific group? What if I concentrated on the roles that various women played in King Philip's War? From previous research, I already had much of the material at hand. All it needed was a little shaping, a little tweaking, and lo and behold, "Women in King Philip's War" became an hour-long presentation which, judging by the judicious questions received from the audience and the favorable comments given--not to mention the number of books purchased at the signing afterwards--was a great success.

My wife, Yolanda, was invited to attend the talk. She enjoyed it (she says, and she's a very candid critic!) and observed that the subject matter was received by the women with enthusiasm. It was she who came up with the idea of my writing a book on the subject.

At first I jibbed at the suggestion. Putting a book together is a lot of work. Even though, as stated, I had much of the material at hand, much more was needed; obtaining it would require hours, nay days! of research. But I soon saw the wisdom of the idea: bringing into prominence the contributions of a segment of the population whose deeds, heroic or otherwise, have too often been ignored or merely glossed over. And to be honest, despite the drudgery (never mind the dust and grime), I actually enjoy research, ferreting out interesting facts and rediscovering authors from the past (many of them sadly neglected) who have written with skill and insight on a particular subject.

And so *Women in King Philip's War* was born.

⁂

I have, insofar as possible, attempted to profile as many Indians as English, and to devote a commensurate amount of space to Indians, both as individuals and as a group. Unfortunately, two ineluctable circumstances of history have made this a daunting task: the Indians had no written language; they wrote nothing down. And (discounting the allies of the English, and those few tribes who attempted to remain neutral) they lost the war; their numbers were drastically reduced: from death by violence, disease, or starvation; from self-exile into other parts of North America; or from being sold into foreign lands as slaves. As a consequence even their oral histories were sorely diminished. Many names of heroic Indian women, many deeds of sacrifice or valor, have been irrevocably lost to us.

⁂

The text comprises three sections. The first is devoted to the three squaw sachems, Awashonks, Weetamoo, and Quaiapen, whose roles of leadership in the war were significant. The story of Mary Rowlandson makes up the second section.

4

It is a story which has often been told, but which is well worth repeating. Consistent with the subject of this book, I have excerpted passages from her narrative that pertain primarily to women, and have added material of my own, both exegetic and explicatory.

The third and final section I have chosen to label "Harpies, Housewives, and Heroines." My edition of *The American Heritage Dictionary of the English Language* defines Harpy, upper case H, as "*Greek Mythology*. One of several loathsome, voracious monsters, having a woman's head and trunk and a bird's tail, wings, and talons" and harpy, lower case h, as 1. a predatory person 2. a shrewish woman." It is the story of the women of Marblehead ("The Gentler Sex?") that prompted me to employ the term--as, I confess, an attention-grabber. It remains for the reader to determine whether the designation, applied to those women, is justified--or whether I should have chosen an even more damning term.

Not all of the other stories in the third section are about heroines (though many are). I've included a few about the special plight of women in the war, so that the title *Women in King Philip's War* refers not only to notable individuals, but also to women in general, both Indian and English. As for actual heroines, there are a number of these, both those whose names are known to us, and those who long ago joined the ranks of "anonymous."

Of course, fortitude and courage come in many guises. Ann Brackett in the face of adversity ("Escape by Needle and Thread") demonstrated one type, Hannah Lyman ("Hurrah for Hannah!") quite another. On the Indian side, squaws, sometimes taking great risks, had their own unique ways of helping in the war effort ("Stratagem and Stealth"). Finally, I've included an example of still another form of heroism, that of simple (and in this instance reciprocal) humanity: a woman, herself enduring great hardship, performing an act of kindness for a woman of the opposing side ("The Milk of Human Kindness").

The Appendices, in effect, make up a fourth section, of miscellaneous subject matter set aside from the main text for various reasons. In Appendix I, I discuss the use of the words "squaw" and "Indian," and the political correctness thereof. Appendix II gives a more comprehensive account of the colonial kitchen, where women settlers spent a great portion of their lives, than is touched upon in the individual stories. Appendix III gives a detailed description of Quaiapen's stone fortress.

Finally, I've provided a brief Time Line (immediately following this Preface) of major events, of significance either to the war in general, or to the lives of the women profiled in the three sections.

Edward Lodi
Middleborough, Massachusetts

Time Line

A Modest Disclaimer on the Matter of Dates

I have attempted to make the following Time Line as accurate as possible. However, certain difficulties obtain.

In the seventeenth century the New Year started on March 25, the date on which it was believed that the Virgin Mary was born. This often leads to confusion and apparent discrepancies. By present-day reckoning, for example, the raid on Lancaster occurred February 10, 1676. But contemporaries might have written it as 1675; others would give the year as 1675 / 76. And there is the little matter of faulty memory. Benjamin Church, with the aid of his son, wrote his memoirs of the war some forty years after it ended; he is known to have confused dates, and to have mixed up the sequence of certain events.

To add to the confusion, there are many factual discrepancies to be found in the records, many disagreements even among those who, participants or merely onlookers, were creating documents at the very time the war raged on, or shortly thereafter.

Then of course there's that old bugaboo, the Gregorian calendar, the calendar we use today, which was introduced by Pope Gregory XIII in 1582--but not adopted by England and the American colonies until 1752. This leads to dates sometimes being given as "Old Style" or "New Style," or worse, not designated as either.

July, 1662: Alexander is forcibly taken by Josiah Winslow to meet with Plymouth officials. Accompanied by **Weetamoo** and others he is then brought to Marshfield as a guest at the home of Josiah and **Penelope Winslow**, where he becomes ill. He later dies. **Weetamoo** and Philip believe he was deliberately poisoned.

July 24, 1671: Amidst signs of unrest and possible preparations for war among the Wampanoags and other tribes, **Awashonks**, together with other leaders, is summoned to Plymouth, where she signs a treaty of submission.

June 15, 1675: **Awashonks** holds a ceremonial dance and council of war. Benjamin Church urges her to remain loyal to Plymouth. However, with the outbreak of war, and Church's inability to communicate further with her, she reluctantly joins with Philip.

June 24: Wampanoags kill nine Swansea settlers. In Rehoboth, they kill Rachel Man and her newborn child. The war has begun.

July 5: Philip arrives at **Weetamoo**'s village; the Pokanokets and Pocassets join forces.

Mid July: Led by Totoson, Wampanoags attack and destroy Old Dartmouth. Josiah Winslow, fearing an Indian attack against Marshfield, sends **Penelope** and their children to Salem.

July 14: Led by Matoonas, Nipmucks attack Mendon (Quinshepauge), killing six settlers, thereby extending the war into Massachusetts Bay Colony.

July 18: In Taunton, Plymouth and Massachusetts Bay Colony troops join forces and march toward **Weetamoo**'s Pocasset.

July 19: Led by James Cudworth, the English forces move into the cedar swamp at Pocasset (present-day Tiverton, Rhode Island) and attempt to engage Philip and about five hundred of his followers. The Wampanoags flee, while inflicting casualties upon the English, who decide not to pursue, hoping that hunger will force the enemy to surrender.

August 1: The Reverend Noah Newman with seventy-five volunteers from Rehoboth and Providence, and fifty Mohegans under Oneco, battle with Philip and **Weetamoo** and their followers at Nipsachuck. **Weetamoo** and her Pocassets break company with Philip and seek refuge with the Narragansetts.

August 2: Captains Thomas Wheeler and Edward Hutchinson (son of Anne Hutchinson, the courageous dissenter banished in 1637 from Massachusetts Bay Colony because of her outspoken religious beliefs), together with men from Brookfield, a score of troopers, and their Indian guides are ambushed by two hundred Indians in present-day New Braintree. They suffer heavy casualties. Hutchinson is mortally wounded. The survivors retreat to Brookfield. Led by Muttaump, Nipmucks lay siege to Brookfield.

August 5: Philip with forty of his warriors and a number of women and children joins the Nipmucks at Menameset.

August 22: Led by Monoco, Nashaways kill seven settlers in Lancaster.

August 30: In Marlborough, Captain Samuel Moseley (privateer turned Indian fighter) and his company (many of whom are former pirates) kidnap friendly Christian Indians (among them James the Printer). The Indians are forcibly marched to Boston, where they are nearly lynched. This action typifies the many persecutions suffered by innocent Indians.

Early September: Drunken English sailors, testing the myth that Indian babies are able to swim at birth, cause the death of the infant son of Squando, sagamore of the Sokokis. This wanton act of cruelty incites the Abenakis of Maine and New Hampshire to rise up against the English. In the Connecticut River Valley Indians attack Deerfield, Hadley, and Northfield.

September 12: At Falmouth (Portland), Maine, Abenakis attack the home of Thomas Wakely, killing six, abducting others; near Casco Bay, English kill a Penobscot in an unprovoked attack.

September 18: In South Deerfield, a thousand Indians attack soldiers and teamsters under the command of Captain

Thomas Lathrop, killing most of them, causing Muddy Brook to be renamed Bloody Brook.

October 1: Abenakis attack the house of Richard (or John?) Tozer in South Berwick, Maine, near Salmon Falls, New Hampshire. They are thwarted by an eighteen-year-old woman and succeed only in killing a three-year-old child and abducting an eleven-year-old.

October 30: Peaceful Christian Indians are forcibly removed to an internment camp on Deer Island, where hundreds die of starvation, illness, and exposure.

December 14: English forces under Josiah Winslow march from Smith's Castle (Wickford, Rhode Island) into Narragansett country. They burn two deserted villages, including that of **Quaiapen**, and kill several Indians, taking others prisoner.

December 19: Under Winslow's command, an army of more than one thousand English and their Mohegan allies attack the Narragansetts' fortified village in the swamp near South Kingston, Rhode Island. After hours of fierce fighting they gain the upper hand and set fire to the wigwams, killing hundreds of women and children. (**Weetamoo** and **Quaiapen** are presumed to have been present.)

December 30: Daniel Gookin sends two Christian Indian spies, Job Kattenanit and James Quannapohit, into Nipmuck country to learn the whereabouts of the enemy.

January 24, 1676: James Quannapohit warns Massachusetts of Indian plans to attack Lancaster, Groton, Marlborough, Sudbury, and Medfield. His warnings are largely ignored.

February 9: Having traveled eighty miles on snowshoes from Menameset (New Braintree), Job Kattenanit wakes Daniel Gookin in Cambridge to warn him that in the morning four hundred Indians will attack Lancaster. The English dispatch messengers to alert Lancaster, Concord, and Marlborough.

February 10: Led by Quinnapin, four hundred Indians attack Lancaster. **Mary Rowlandson** and three of her children, along with twenty others, are taken hostage.

February 21: Less than twenty miles from Boston, several hundred Nipmucks and Narragansetts led by Monoco attack Medfield (having, despite the presence of nearly two hundred soldiers and militiamen, infiltrated the night before by hiding in barns and trees); they withdraw only after killing seventeen English, abducting others, and destroying thirty-two buildings.

March 2: Major Savage with six hundred men leaves Brookfield to attack the Indians at Menemesit. Finding the villages deserted, he sets out in pursuit of the group (in which **Mary Rowlandson** is held captive) led by Muttaump. Indians begin a series of attacks on Groton.

March 6: Arriving at the Millers River, Major Savage abandons the pursuit of Muttaump.

March 12: Led by Totoson, ten Indians attack and destroy Clark's Garrison on the Eel River, less than three miles from Plymouth itself, killing Mrs. Clark and ten others, and taking away guns, powder and lead, and many pounds sterling.

March 26: A company of sixty-three English soldiers under Captain Michael Pierce and twenty Christian Indians under Captain Amos are ambushed by Narragansetts at the Pawtucket (Blackstone) River in present-day Central Falls, north of Providence. Most of the English and many of the Christian Indians are killed.

March 28: Fifteen hundred Indians attack and destroy Old Rehoboth.

March 29: Narragansetts attack Providence, eventually burning more than a hundred buildings, including the home of Roger Williams.

April 2: Connecticut troops and their Indian allies capture Canonchet; he is executed the following day at Stonington.

April 3: The Massachusetts Council sends Nepanet (Tom Dublet) to the Nipmucks at Wachusett with a letter suggesting peace negotiations and the ransom of captives, including **Mary Rowlandson.**

April 12: Nepanet returns to Boston with the Indians' reply to the letter from the Massachusetts Council; the Nipmucks refuse to discuss peace.

Mid April: Indians raid Bridgewater, Billerica, Scituate, Andover, and Hingham.

April 21: Led by Muttaump, fifteen hundred Indians attack Sudbury and, despite the arrival of soldiers from neighboring communities, inflict heavy casualties. Fifty English led by Captain Samuel Wadsworth with Captain Samuel Brocklebank are ambushed at Green Hill. Both captains, along with thirty of their men, are killed. Even though the Indians win the battle, this is a turning point in the war. The Indians fail to drive the English out or to destroy the town. They return to their base demoralized.

May: Governor Edmund Andros of New York sends sloops to Newport, Rhode Island, to transport English refugees for resettlement in Long Island and elsewhere in New York.

May 2: Upon the payment of twenty pounds ransom by John Hoar, **Mary Rowlandson** is freed in Princeton, Massachusetts.

May 3: At Bradford, Thomas Kemble (Kimbal) is killed and his wife and five children taken captive by Simon and others, who had earlier killed a settler at Haverhill. The captives are later released upon the intercession of Wannalancet.

May 18: Led by Captain William Turner, one hundred and fifty men and boys on horseback leave Hatfield to attack Indians encamped at Peskeompscut (the Upper Falls) in Montague.

May 19: Turner's company attack the Indians as they sleep in their wigwams and, taking no prisoners, massacre a hundred or more, including many women and children. The English are then attacked by Indians from nearby camps. More than forty English, including Turner, are killed.

May 20: Indians attack Scituate. **Mrs. Ewell**, who has been baking bread, flees the house. She returns sometime later, to find her bread removed from the oven and her infant grandson unharmed.

June: Connecticut volunteers kill or capture numerous Indians in Narragansett country east of the Pawcatuck River.

June 6: Benjamin Church arrives in Plymouth. The General Court appoints him as field commander, to raise an army to consist of one hundred and fifty English and fifty Indians.

June 9: Captain Henchman with his troops and Christian Indians surprises a band of Indians fishing near Lancaster, killing seven and capturing twenty-nine. Among the captured are Muttaump's wife and Sagamore Sam's wife and children.

June 11: Peter, son of **Awashonks**, with a letter from Captain Church, proceeds to Plymouth to negotiate the surrender of **Awashonks** and her Sakonnets.

June 30: Encouraged by Benjamin Church, **Awashonks** and about ninety of her people give themselves up to William Bradford at Pocasset. He orders them to move on to Sandwich. Afterwards, many of her warriors serve under Church.

July 2: In Smithfield, Rhode Island, Major Talcott's contingent of English and Indians, assisted by Captain Newbury, kill more than 170 men, women, and children. Among those killed are Stonewall John and **Quaiapen**, the Old Queen. In Cambridge, a number of Indians, among them James the Printer, give themselves up.

July 31: Men from Bridgewater encounter a group of Indians attempting to cross the Taunton River. They kill several, including Philip's uncle Unkompoin, and capture Philip's sister (**Amie**, wife of Tispaquin, or possibly another sister, whose name is unknown).

August 1: Church spies Philip on the opposite bank of the Taunton River. Although Philip escapes, his wife, **Wootonekanuske**, and their nine-year-old son are captured.

August 6: Men from Taunton encounter a number of Indians in present-day Norton and capture more than two dozen. Although she eludes capture, **Weetamoo** drowns while attempting to cross the Taunton River.

August 9: Using subterfuge, Simon and five others access the Brackett settlement on Casco Neck. Of the English, eleven men are killed; twenty-three women and children are killed or taken captive (among the latter **Ann Brackett**).

August 12: At Mount Hope, Church and his men attack Philip's camp. Alderman shoots and kills Philip. Anawan escapes with about fifty followers.

August 13: Indians attack and destroy Richard Hammond's trading post in Woolwich, Maine, killing fifteen.

August 14: Indians attack and destroy the fortress at the Clarke and Lake Trading Post in Arrowsic, Maine.

August 16: Quinnapin is captured and taken to Newport.

August 17: Plymouth Colony observes a Day of Thanksgiving. Philip's head is paraded throughout Plymouth, then placed on a pole on the palisade on Fort Hill for public display, where it remains for more than twenty years.

August 25: Quinnapin, along with his brother Sunkeejunasuc, is executed in Newport.

August 28: Church surprises Anawan in Squannakonk Swamp in present-day Rehoboth. Anawan surrenders without a fight and hands over Philip's wampum belts.

September: Hundreds of Indian prisoners are sold into slavery or domestic servitude. Hundreds more are hanged or shot.

September 6: Tispaquin surrenders to Church at Agawam (Wareham). Despite Church's promises to the contrary, he is executed in Plymouth and his wife, **Amie**, and son sold into slavery. In Dover, New Hampshire, Major Walderne betrays four hundred Indians who are seeking peace, allowing them to be seized by forces commanded by Captains Joseph Sill, William Hathorne, and Charles Frost. He sends two hundred warriors as captives by ship to Boston, where many are killed or sold into slavery.

September 7: The Reverends Samuel Arnold and John Cotton sign a letter advocating a sentence of death for **Wootonekanuske**, Philip's wife, and their nine-year-old son.

September 26: Monoco and Sagamore Sam, along with others, are hanged on Boston Common.

March, 1677: The first shipload of food from England and Ireland arrives in Boston to help feed starving refugees.

March 20: Philip's nine-year-old son is sold into slavery.

May 14: Led by Mugg Hegone and Simon, more than one hundred Indians attack the garrison at Black Point (which they had previously taken, but later abandoned).

May 16: Mugg Hegone is killed during the siege at Black Point. Demoralized, the Indians leave the area.

Summer: Indians attack ports along the coast of Maine, seizing thirteen ships.

August 12: Fearful that the Mohawks will enter the war, the Abenakis sign a peace treaty, ending hostilities for the short run.

"In a sense, King Philip's War never ended. In other times, in other places, its painful wounds would be reopened, its vicious words spoken again."--Jill Lepore, The Name of War

The Squaw Sachems

Awashonks

Awashonks herself in a foaming sweat was leading the dance.--Thomas Church, Entertaining Passages Relating to Philip's War *(printed by B. Green in 1716)*

A New Bedford whale ship was named Awashonks, *for this well-known woman who held domain not far from that port.--Allan Forbes, compiler,* Other Indian Events of New England, *(Boston: The State Street Trust Company of Boston, 1941)*

Shortly before the start of King Philip's War the Indian leader Awashonks found herself on the horns of a dilemma, or if you prefer an alternative cliché, she was caught between a rock and a hard place, or the devil and the deep blue sea; she was damned if she did and damned if she didn't.

Why belabor the point?

Only in order to emphasize her hapless plight, the helplessness, and seeming hopelessness, of her position.

The Sakonnets, a small tribe affiliated with the Wampanoags, occupied a compact but significant area in the southwestern corner of Plymouth Colony: a peninsula on the northeast side of Narragansett Bay that is now Little Compton, Rhode Island. At the outbreak of hostilities in 1675 Awashonks was their squaw sachem, a position she had held for a number of years.

Although she would prove to be a major player in the war, few details of her life have been preserved; we know neither the year of her birth nor the year of her death, nor her age at the time of the war. We know that "she usually spent her summers in Falmouth making an occasional excursion to Gay Head on the Vineyard, where it is believed she had friends."[from *Other Indian Events of New England*, compiled by Allan Forbes and issued by the State Street Trust Company of Boston in 1941.] She was the widow of Tolony and the sister of Tokamona, who was killed by Narragansetts in 1674. Her husband in 1674 was

Wewayewitt (of whom, except for that one fact, nothing else, apparently, was ever recorded).

In 1671, during a period of unrest--when Awashonks, along with other sachems in Plymouth Colony, were believed to be plotting against those Indians among them who had converted to Christianity--the Court at Plymouth summoned her to appear before them, both to affirm her loyalty to the Colony and to surrender her firearms. After initially defying the English, on July 24 Awashonks appeared before the authorities and signed a treaty of submission. "There is in existence a copy of a letter written by her [through an interpreter] at this time and addressed to Governor Prince of Massachusetts [Thomas Prence, governor of Plymouth Colony] in which she explained that she intended to send in all six of her guns, but that two of them were so large the messengers were unable to carry them and that 'since then an Indian, known by the name of Broad-faced-will stole one of them out of the wigwam in the night, and is run away with it to Mount Hope." [*Other Indian Events.*]

From what we know of Awashonks, she was a capable and peace-loving leader, respected by her people and for the most part (albeit reluctantly) well disposed toward the English. Or if not well disposed, she must at least have recognized the futility of engaging them in a bloody conflict from which she and her fellow Sakonnets had little to gain, everything to lose. Philip, sachem of the Pokanokets, Great Sachem of all the Wampanoags, was a near neighbor in Mount Hope (now Bristol, Rhode Island), as was Weetamoo, Philip's sister-in-law and squaw sachem of another small tribe of Wampanoags, the Pocassets, who occupied territory in what is now present-day Tiverton, Rhode Island and Fall River, Massachusetts.

Also close by were the powerful Narragansetts, traditional and bitter enemies of the Wampanoags.

As of 1674 Awashonks had a new, and immediate, neighbor: Benjamin Church, who with his wife and family was one of a handful of English settlers in the area that would one day become Little Compton.

Sachems, whether male or female, though wielding great authority and making decisions of life and death, did not enjoy absolute power; they ruled at the sufferance of their people. In the weeks of unrest leading up to the war, Awashonks was under great pressure from many, perhaps the majority, of her young warriors to join Philip's cause to drive the English out of New England. Even so, she might have been able to restrain them and remain neutral had not fate intervened.

The following, with minor editorial changes, is taken from John S. C. Abbott's *History of King Philip, Sovereign Chief of the Wampanoags*, published in 1857.

⁂

"Upon the eastern shore of Narragansett Bay there was a small tribe of Indians called the Sakonnets. A woman, Awashonks, was sachem of the tribe, and the bravest warriors were prompt to do homage to her power. Captain Benjamin Church and a few other colonists had purchased lands of her, and had settled upon fertile spots along the shores of the bay. Awashonks was on very friendly terms with Captain Church. Though there were three hundred warriors obedient to her command, that was but a feeble force compared with the troops which could be raised both by Philip and by the English. She was therefore anxious to remain neutral.

"This however could not be. The war was such that all dwelling in the midst of its ravages must choose their side.

"Philip sent six ambassadors to engage Awashonks in his interest. She immediately assembled all her counselors to deliberate upon the momentous question, and also took the very wise precaution to send for Captain Church. He hastened to her residence, and found several hundred of her subjects collected and engaged in a furious dance. The forest rang with their shouts, the perspiration dripped from their limbs, and they were already wrought to a pitch of intense excitement.

Awashonks herself led in the dance, and her graceful figure appeared to great advantage as it was contrasted with the gigantic muscular development of her warriors.

"Immediately upon Captain Church's arrival the dance ceased. Awashonks sat down, called her chiefs [among them Nompash, her kinsman and principal counselor] and the Wampanoag ambassadors around her, and then invited Captain Church to take a conspicuous seat in the midst of the group. She then, in a speech of queenly courtesy, informed Captain Church that King Philip had sent six of his men to solicit her to enter into a confederacy against the English, and that he stated, through these ambassadors, that the English had raised a great army, and were about to invade his territories for the extermination of the Wampanoags. The conference was long and intensely exciting. Awashonks called upon the Wampanoag ambassadors to come forward.

"They were marked men, dressed in the highest embellishments of barbaric warfare. Their faces were painted. Their hair was trimmed in the fashion of the crests of the ancient helmets. Their knives and tomahawks were sharp and glittering. They all had guns, and horns and pouches abundantly supplied with shot and bullets.

"Captain Church, however, was manifestly gaining the advantage, and the Wampanoag ambassadors, baffled and enraged, were anxious to silence their antagonist with the bludgeon. The Indians began to take sides furiously, and hot words and threatening gestures were abundant. Awashonks was very evidently inclined to adhere to the English. She at last, in the face of the ambassadors, declared to Captain Church that Philip's message to her was that he would send his men over privately to shoot the cattle and burn the houses of the English who were within her territories, and thus induce the English to fall in vengeance upon her, whom they would undoubtedly suppose to be the author of the mischief.

"This so enraged Captain Church that he quite forgot his customary prudence. Turning to the Wampanoag ambassadors he exclaimed, 'You are infamous wretches, thirsting for the blood of your English neighbors, who have never injured you, but who, on the contrary, have always treated you with kindness.'

"Then, addressing Awashonks, he very inconsiderately advised her to knock the six Wampanoags on the head, and then throw herself upon the protection of the English. The Indian queen, more discreet than her advisor, dismissed the ambassadors unharmed, but informing them that she should look to the English as her friends and protectors.

"Captain Church, exulting in this success, which took three hundred warriors from the enemy and added them to the English force, set out for Plymouth. At parting, he advised Awashonks to remain faithful to the English whatever might happen, and to keep, with all her warriors, within the limits of the Sakonnet. He promised to return to her again in a few days."

[Unfortunately the vicissitudes of war prevented Church from returning to Awashonks as promised. Meanwhile, under pressure from her young warriors, and from Philip himself, she with her people joined with Philip in common cause against the English. Abbott picks up the story a year later, in 1676:]

"The latter part of July, Captain Church was placed in command of a force to search for Philip, who, with a small band of faithful followers, had returned to the region of Mount Hope. Captain Church went from Plymouth to Wood's Hole in Falmouth, and there engaged two friendly Indians to paddle him in a canoe across Buzzard's Bay, and along the shore to Rhode Island. As he was rounding the neck of land called Sakonnet Point, he saw a number of Indians fishing from the rocks.

"Believing that these Indians were in heart attached to the English, and that they had been forced to unite with Philip, he resolved to make efforts to detach them from the confederacy. The Indians on the shore seemed also to seek an interview, and by signs invited them to land. Captain Church, who was as

Captain Church's visit to the Saconets.

prudent as he was intrepid, called to two of the Indians to go down upon a point of cleared land where there was no room for an ambush. He then landed, and, leaving one of the Indians to take care of the canoe, and the other to act as a sentinel, advanced to meet the Indians.

"One of the two Indians, who was named George [called Honest George by the English], could speak English perfectly well. He told Captain Church that his tribe was weary of the war; that they were in a state of great suffering, and that they were very anxious to return to a state of friendly alliance with the English. He said that if the past could be pardoned, his tribe was ready not only to relinquish all acts of hostility, but to take up arms against Philip.

"Captain Church promised to meet them again in two days at Richmond's Farm, upon this long neck of land. He then hastened to Rhode Island, procured an interview with the governor [William Coddington], and endeavored to obtain authority to enter into a treaty with the Indians. The governor would not give his assent, affirming that it was an act of madness in Captain Church to trust himself among the Sakonnets. Nevertheless, Church, true to his engagement, took with him an interpreter, and embarking in a canoe, reached the spot at the appointed time.

"Here he found Awashonks with several of her followers. As his canoe touched the shore, she advanced to meet him, and, with a smile of apparent friendliness, extended her hand. They walked together a short distance from the shore, when suddenly a large party of Indians, painted and decorated in warlike array, and armed to the teeth, sprang up from an ambush in the high grass, and surrounded them.

"Church, undismayed, turned to Awashonks, and said, indignantly, 'I supposed that your object in inviting me to this interview was peace.'

"'And so it is,' Awashonks replied.

"'Why, then,' Captain Church continued, 'are your warriors here with arms in their hands?'

"Awashonks appeared embarrassed, and replied, 'What weapons do you wish them to lay aside?'

"The Indian warriors scowled angrily, and deep mutterings were passed among them. Captain Church, seeing his helpless situation, very proudly replied, 'I only wish them to lay aside their guns, which is a proper formality when friends meet to treat for peace.'

"Hearing this, the Indians laid aside their guns, and quietly seated themselves around their queen and Captain Church. An interesting and perilous interview now ensued. Awashonks accused the English of provoking her to hostilities when she had wished to live in friendship with them. At one moment the Indians would seem to be in a towering rage, and again perfectly pleasant, and almost affectionate.

"Captain Church happened to allude to one of the battles between the English and the Indians. Immediately one of the warriors, foaming with rage, sprang toward him, brandishing his tomahawk, and threatening to sink it in his brain, declaring that Captain Church had slain his brother in that battle. Captain Church replied that his brother was the aggressor, and that, if he had remained at home, as Captain Church had advised him to do, his life would have been spared. At this the irate warrior immediately calmed down, and all was peace again.

"As a result of the interview, Awashonks promised to ally herself in friendship with the English upon condition that Church should obtain the pardon of her tribe for all past offenses. The chief captain of her warriors [her son Peter] then approached Captain Church with great stateliness, and said, 'Sir, if you will please to accept of me and my men, and will be our captain, we will fight for you, and will help you to the head of King Philip before the Indian corn be ripe.' At this all the other warriors clashed their weapons and murmured applause.

"Church then proposed that five Indians should accompany him through the woods to the governor to secure the ratification of the treaty. Awashonks objected to this, saying that the party would inevitably be intercepted on the way by Philip's warriors, and all would be slain. She proposed, however, that Captain Church should go to Rhode Island, obtain a small vessel, and then take her ambassadors around Cape Cod to Plymouth.

"Captain Church obtained a small vessel in Newport Harbor, and sailed for the point. When he arrived there the wind was directly ahead, and blowing almost a gale. As the storm increased, finding himself unable to land, he returned to Newport. Being a man of deep religious sensibilities, he considered this disappointment as an indication of divine disapproval, and immediately relinquished the enterprise.

"Just at this time Major William Bradford [Jr., son of the second governor of Plymouth Colony] arrived in the vicinity of the present town of Fall River with a large force of soldiers. This region was then called Pocasset, and was within the territory of Queen Weetamoo. Captain Church immediately then took a canoe, and again visited Awashonks. He informed her of the arrival of Major Bradford, urged her to keep all her people at home lest they should be assailed by these troops, and assured her that if she would visit Major Bradford in his encampment she should be received with kindness, and a treaty of peace would be concluded. The next morning, Major Bradford, with his whole force, marched down the Tiverton shore, and encamped at a place called Punkatese, halfway between Pocasset and Sakonnet Point.

"Awashonks collected her warriors and repaired to Punkatese to meet the English. Major Bradford received her with severity and suspicion, which appears to have been quite unjustifiable. Awashonks offered to surrender her warriors to his service if they could be under the command of Captain Church, in whom both she and they reposed perfect confidence. This offer was peremptorily declined, and she was haughtily commanded to appear at Sandwich, where the governor resided, within six days. The queen, mortified by this unfriendly reception, appealed to Captain Church. He, also, was much chagrined, but advised her to obey, assuring her that the governor would cordially assent to her views. The Indians, somewhat reassured, now commenced their march to Sandwich [which extended the full width of Cape Cod, from Massachusetts Bay on the north to Nantucket Sound on the south, Buzzards Bay to the west, and Barnstable to the east, and included what is now the town of Bourne], under the protection of a flag of truce [carried by Jack Haven, a Cape Cod Indian].

"The next morning Major Bradford embarked his army in canoes, and crossed to Mount Hope in search of King Philip. It was late at night before they reached the Mount, and the fires blazing in the woods showed that the Indians were collecting in large numbers. Meeting, however, with no foe, they marched on to Rehoboth. Here Captain Church, taking an Indian for a guide, set out for Plymouth to intercede for his friends, the Sakonnet Indians. The governor received him with great cordiality. Captain Church, highly gratified, took with him three or four men as a bodyguard, and hastened to Sandwich. Disappointed in not finding Awashonks there, he went to Agawam, in the present town of Wareham; still not finding her, he crossed the Mattapoiset River, and ascended a bluff which commanded a wide prospect of Buzzard's Bay.

"As they stood upon the bluff, they heard a loud murmuring noise coming from the concealed shore [Pope's Beach] at a little distance. Creeping cautiously along, they peered over a low cliff, and saw a large number of Indians, of all ages and sexes, engaged upon the beach in the wildest scene of festivities. Some were running races on horseback; some playing at football; some were catching eels and flatfish; and others plunging and frolicking in the waves.

"Uncertain whether they were enemies or friends, Captain Church retired some distance into a thicket, and then hallooed to them. Two young Indians, hearing the shout, left the rest of their company to see from whence it came. They came close upon Captain Church before he discovered himself to them. As soon as they saw Captain Church, with two or three men around him, all well armed, they, in a panic, endeavored to retreat. He succeeded, however, in retaining them, and in disarming their fears.

"From them he learned that the party consisted of Awashonks and her tribe. He then sent word to Awashonks that he intended to sup with her that evening, and to lodge in her camp that night. The queen immediately made preparations to receive him and his companions with all due respect. Captain Church and his men, mounted on horseback, rode down to the beach. The Indians gathered around them with shouts of welcome. They were conducted to a pleasant tent, open toward the sea, and were provided with a luxurious supper of fried fish. The supper consisted of three courses; a young bass in one dish, eels and flatfish in a second, and shellfish in a third; but there was neither bread nor salt.

"By the time supper was over it was night, serene and moonless, yet brilliant with stars. The still waters of Buzzard's Bay lay like a burnished mirror, reflecting the sparkling canopy above in a corresponding arch below. The unbroken forest frowned along the shore, sublime in its solitude, and from its depths could only be heard the lonely cry of the birds of darkness.

"The Indians collected an enormous pile of pine knots and the resinous boughs of the fir tree. Men, women, and children all contributed to enlarge the gigantic heap, and when the torch was touched, a bonfire of amazing splendor blazed far and wide over the forest and the bay. This was the introductory act to a drama where peace and war were blended. All the Indians, old and young, gathered around the fire. Awashonks, with the oldest men and women of the tribe, kneeling down in a circle, formed the first ring; next behind then came all the most distinguished warriors, armed and arrayed in all the gorgeous panoply of warfare; then came a motley multitude of the common mass of men, women, and children.

"At an appointed signal, Awashonks's chief captain stepped forward from the circle, danced with frantic gesture around the fire, drew a brand from the flames, and, calling it the name of a tribe hostile to the English, belabored it with bludgeon and tomahawk. He then drew out another and another, until all the tribes hostile to the English had been named, assailed, and exterminated. Reeking with perspiration, and exhausted by his frenzied efforts, he retired within the ring. Another chief then came out and reenacted the same scene, endeavoring to surpass his predecessor in the fierceness and fury of his efforts.

"In this way all the chiefs took what they considered as their oath of fidelity to the English. The chief captain then came forward to Captain Church, and, presenting him with a fine musket, informed him that all the warriors were henceforth subject to his command. Captain Church immediately drew out a number of the ablest warriors, and the next morning, before the break of day, set out with them for Plymouth.

"It is said that when King Philip, in the midst of his accumulating disasters, learned that the Sakonnet tribe had abandoned his cause and had gone over to the English, he was never known to smile again. He knew that his doom was now sealed, and that nothing remained for him but to be hunted as a wild beast of the forest for the remainder of his days."

Awashonks's son Peter, also known as Mamaneway, was with Benjamin Church at the battle in which Philip was killed. Several of the Sakonnet warriors continued to serve under Church long after the end of King Philip's War. Lightfoot, for example, became a sergeant and was with Church in the Eastern Expedition to Casco in 1689. Awashonks's ultimate fate is unknown; we do know that she was still alive in 1683.

In July of that year, Awashonks, her son Peter, and her daughter Betty were charged by the Plymouth authorities with the crime of infanticide. Evidently Betty had given birth to an illegitimate child. Awashonks and Peter helped to bury the baby, which they stated had been stillborn. Ultimately all three were acquitted of the crime of murder, though Betty was found guilty of fornication.

This unfortunate episode demonstrates the diminution of Awashonks's power as a ruler, and the loss of independence by the Indian tribes that survived the war. Formerly, the Indians had been more or less autonomous; now they were subject to English law, and to English interference in their daily lives.

Samuel D. Drake, in *Biography and History of the Indians of North America*, published in Boston in 1841, gives us additional information about Awashonks's people and what the future held for them:

"It is said that Awashonks had two sons; the younger was William Mommynewit, who was put to a grammar school and learned the Latin language, and was intended for college, but was prevented by being seized with the palsy. Some of the Indian soldiers requested liberty to pursue the Narragansetts and other enemy Indians, immediately after they had captured Philip's wife and son. 'They said the Narragansetts were great rogues, and they wanted to be revenged on them, for killing some of their relations' (Awashonks's brother Tokamona and others).

"About 1700 there were one hundred Indian men of the Sakonnet tribe, and the general assembly appointed Numphas their captain, who lived to be an old man, and died about 1748, after the taking of Cape Breton in 1745. At the commencement of the eighteenth century, they made quite a respectable religious congregation; they had a meeting house of their own, in which they were instructed by Reverend Mr. Billings, once a month, on Sundays. They had a steady preacher among themselves, whose name was John Simon, a man of strong mind.

"About 1750 a very distressing fever carried off many of the tribe, and in 1803 there were not above ten in [Little] Compton, their principal residence."

In the late nineteenth century, in an area of Little Compton known as Wilbur Wood, a boulder was engraved in honor of Awashonks. It reads: "In memory of Awashonks Queen of Sogkonate & friend of the white man."

Weetamoo

Weetamoo: a severe and proud dame she was, bestowing every day in dressing herself neat as much time as any of the gentry of the land: powdering her hair, and painting her face, going with necklaces, with jewels in her ears, and bracelets upon her hands: when she had dressed herself, her work was to make girdles of wampum and beads.--Mary Rowlandson, The Narrative of the Captivity and Restoration of Mrs. Mary Rowlandson

The name "Weetamoe" came into international prominence when one of the yachts that contended for the honor of defending the America's Cup, *in 1930, bore the name of this influential Wampanoag Indian queen. Perhaps the owners of the famous racing craft selected this name in the hopes that she might battle the English as stubbornly as did the Queen Sachem Weetamoe in King Philip's War.--Allan Forbes, compiler,* Some Indian Events of New England, *(Boston: The State Street Trust Company of Boston, 1934)*

It is regrettable that Hollywood, in its golden age, failed to make a motion picture based on the life of Weetamoo. If a major studio had undertaken the task, surely the resulting movie would have rivaled *Cleopatra* in scope. Imagine the melodrama, the tragedy, the romance! The cast of thousands! The scenic splendor, the spectacle, the historic sweep, the peacetime intrigue and wartime adventure!

❧

Born around 1635, Weetamoo was the daughter of, and successor to, Corbitant, sachem of the Pocassets. "One of her camps was situated a little way from the shore on a high hill, north of the old Howland Ferry or Bridge, where now stands the stone bridge over the Sakonnet River. Her other domicile was south of Fall River, on the north side of Pocasset Cedar Swamp, between South Watuppa Pond and the heights that look down Mount Hope Bay. Near here was an Indian colony, for many years called Indian Town." [*Some Indian Events of New England*]

She was the older sister of Wootonekanuske, Philip's wife. In Algonquin, Weetamoo means "Sweet Heart." There is supreme irony in her name; she was married five times, and so was presumably the sweetheart of at least some of her husbands. Yet the tragic events of her life might justifiably have caused her "sweet" heart to turn bitter.

Her first husband was Wequiquinequa. After his death, in 1652 she married Alexander (Wamsutta), Philip's older brother, and successor to his father Massasoit as Great Sachem of the Wampanoags. In 1659 Weetamoo entered a complaint in

43

the Plymouth Court against Wamsutta, claiming that he sold land belonging to her without paying her; she made a similar complaint in 1662, shortly before his death, concerning another sale of land.

Alexander died under unfortunate, and mysterious, circumstances in 1662. After being forcibly removed from his camp at Lake Monponsett by Josiah Winslow and brought to Duxbury by the Plymouth authorities, he succumbed to an apparent stomach ailment. Philip and Weetamoo, however, believed that he had been deliberately poisoned by the English.

She next married Quequequanchett, about whom little is known. Her fourth husband was Petananuet (also known as Peter Nunnuit). This marriage ended in June of 1675, when Petananuet, sympathetic to the English cause, warned Benjamin Church of Philip's warlike intentions. There is some disagreement among historians as to whether Weetamoo willingly joined Philip, or whether she was coerced (by circumstances, and the impetuosity of her young warriors) into doing so. The following (with minor changes) is taken from John S. C. Abbott's *History of King Philip, Sovereign Chief of the Wampanoags.*

"Just north of Little Compton, in the region now occupied by the upper part of Tiverton, and by Fall River, the Pocasset tribe of Indians dwelt. Weetamoo, the former bride of Alexander, was a princess of this tribe. Upon the death of her husband and the accession of Philip to the sovereignty of the Wampanoags, she had returned to her parental home, and was now queen of the tribe. Her power was about equal to that of Awashonks, and she could lead three or four hundred warriors into the field. Captain Church immediately proceeded to her court, as he deemed it exceedingly important to detach her, if possible, from the coalition.

"He found her upon a high hill at a short distance from the shore. But few of her people were with her, and she appeared reserved and very melancholy. She acknowledged that all her warriors had gone across the water to Philip's war dance, though she said that it was against her will. She was, however, brooding over her past injuries, and was eager to join Philip in any measures of revenge. Captain Church had hardly arrived at Plymouth before the wonderful successes of Philip so encouraged the Indians that Weetamoo, with alacrity and burning zeal, joined the coalition."

Subsequent events are related by Daniel Strock, Jr. (in *Pictorial History of King Philip's War*, published in 1851, from which the following, with minor changes, is taken):

"Ascertaining the condition of his kinswoman, Philip sent an embassy to her, which had the desired effect. The Plymouth authorities, as she supposed, not content with killing her first husband, had seduced her second one [Strock was obviously unaware of her other marriages], so that no friend was left but Philip. No longer able to remain neutral, she joined her relative, and accompanied him in his wanderings about Pocasset, until his escape from that place, July 30, 1675. From this time her movements are so identified with those of Philip, as to render the tracing of them extremely difficult.

"During that summer she became separated from the main body of the Indians, and was received by Ninigret [sachem of the Eastern Niantics, and brother of the squaw sachem Quaiapen] as his guest. For the crime of harboring her, this chief was called to account by the Plymouth court, but he eluded their demands, and Weetamoo soon after escaped to the Narragansetts. Intelligence of this reached the colonists, and was one cause of their determination to invade the Narragansett country. It is not known whether Weetamoo was at the fort [in the swamp near South Kingston, Rhode Island, attacked on December 19, 1675, by more than one thousand English and their Mohegan allies; it remains the bloodiest battle ever fought in New England] at the time of the massacre [those killed by the English included hundreds of women and children, many of them burned to death in their wigwams] but the probability is that she was.

"About this time Weetamoo joined herself with Quinnapin, a famous chief of the Narragansetts, with whom she appears to have lived in great amity [along with his two other wives]. Mrs. Rowlandson, during her captivity, frequently met with her [the captive Mary Rowlandson was Quinnapin's and Weetamoo's slave], and the description she gives of the Indian queen, spiced with hatred, and perhaps a little of female jealousy, is somewhat entertaining. 'My master had three squaws, living sometimes with one, and sometimes with another--one was Weetamoo, with whom I had lived and served all this while.

"'A severe and proud dame was she, bestowing every day, in dressing herself, near as much time as any of the gentry of the land--powdering her hair and painting her face, going with her necklaces, with jewels in her ears, and bracelets upon her hands. When she had dressed herself, her work was to make girdles of wampum and beads.'

"Such is the substance of Weetamoo's history, as handed to us by her enemy. She appears to have been a woman of much energy, faithful in the cause which she considered right, and sincerely desirous of the welfare of her subjects. Her disposition was amiable until soured by misfortune and injury; and the affection by which she was regarded by her people will appear in the subsequent narrative. The only crime that could be alleged against her was attachment to the cause of Philip; but for this she was hunted from place to place with unrelenting hatred, a price was set upon her head, and whole tribes were destroyed who were guilty of or were suspected of having harbored her.

"Weetamoo had shared the triumphs of Philip; she also shared his misfortunes. When, by intestine divisions, his power was destroyed among the Nipmucks, the queen, like her ally, seems to have been deserted by most of her followers, and like him also she sought refuge in her own country. On the 6th of August, 1676, she arrived upon the western bank of Teticut [actually, the Taunton] River, in Mattapoiset [in Swansea], with twenty-six men, the remainder, numbering two hundred and seventy, having deserted her or been slain in battle. Intelligence of her situation was conveyed to the colonists, as usual, by a deserter, who offered to conduct a party to capture her.

"Twenty men immediately volunteered, glad of the opportunity of capturing the one who was 'next to Philip in respect of the mischief that had been done.' The party proceeded with caution until, guided by the deserter, they reached Weetamoo's position. The surprise was complete. The Indians made no resistance, and had no time to attempt an escape. All were captured except Weetamoo.

"Over the fate of this woman there hangs a singular mystery, which the investigations of earnest inquirers have not been able to explain. [William] Hubbard's account [*A Narrative of the Troubles with the Indians in New-England*, published in Boston in 1677] is as follows: 'Intending to make an escape from the danger, she attempted to get over a river [the mouth of the Taunton River], or arm of the sea near by upon a raft, or some pieces of broken wood; but, whether tired and spent with swimming, or starved with cold and hunger, she was found, stark naked, in Mattapoiset, not far from the water side, which made some think she was first half drowned, and so ended her wretched life.'

"Whether she was first 'half drowned,' whether she was murdered by her people, or whether she met her death in any other way, equally violent, cannot now be ascertained.

"If the tragic story of this princess ended here, it would be well. But the colonists found her naked body by the water's edge. Their enemy was taken at last; yet she was dead, and more than that, her corpse was the corpse of a woman. Surely they would bury it, if not with magnanimity, yet with decency, since the manly heart wars not on the dead. On the contrary, they indulged in taunts over the body, cut off the head, and after carrying it to Taunton, set it upon a pole.

"Here it was recognized by some of the prisoners, who, assembling around it, gave expression to their grief in cries and lamentations. Mournful proof of the love which these poor creatures bore to their unfortunate princess. Yet so bitter was the feeling against the Indians, that [Increase] Mather, several months after this occurrence, denominated this act of the Indian captives 'a most horrid and diabolical lamentation.'

"Weetamoo was among the last of Philip's friends, and although we have no account of the manner in which he received the news of her death, yet there can be little doubt that it affected him deeply. Perhaps his subsequent visit to Pocasset was occasioned by the grief he felt for one who had ever been faithful to his interests."

Quaiapen
(the Old Queen)

Female chiefs were called saunks *by the Indians, which signified wife of the sachem; but writers, being ignorant of that fact, thought it a proper name of a particular person, and hence the appellations of* Snuke, Sunke, Snake *etc. applied to Magnus [Quaiapen].--Samuel D. Drake,* Biography and History of the Indians of North America

Just how old Quaiapen was in 1675, at the outbreak of the war, is not known. We know that her brother, Ninigret, sachem of the Eastern Niantics; was born in 1600.

Although she was one of the six principal sachems of the Narragansetts, she herself was an Eastern Niantic, having married a Narragansett. In the war she sided with Philip; her brother at first maintained neutrality, but eventually joined with the English. She lived in Exeter, Rhode Island, at a natural fortress ("Queen's Fort") which consisted of glacial rocks connected by stone walls erected by Stonewall John (Nawwhan), a Narragansett who had learned masonry from the English. (He also planned and built the fortifications for the Narragansett fort near South Kingston, site of the Great Swamp Fight, or Massacre.)

Unfortunately, we do not know much about Quaiapen's exact movements during the war, or what exactly her leadership role, in regard to military actions, may have been. As always, we are hindered by the fact that the English kept written records (though not necessarily accurate), whereas the Indians did not.

The following, with a number of changes and omissions, is an excerpt from *Soldiers in King Philip's War*, by George Madison Bodge, Third Edition, published in Boston in 1906. It is an account of events that occurred a few days before the Great Swamp Fight near South Kingston, Rhode Island.

"On December 14th, 1675, General Josiah Winslow, Governor of Plymouth Colony, moved his whole force, except Captain [James] Oliver's company, which kept garrison [at Smith's Castle, in Wickford], out through the country to the westward, and burned the town of the sachem Ahmus, and the 'Quarters' of Quaiapen, Magnus, or Matantuck, as her Indian name was understood by the English, 'Old Queen' or

'Sunke Squaw,' as she was called by them. She was the widow of Mriksah, or Makanno, son of Canonicus.

"Her dominions were in the present towns of South and North Kingston and Exeter; and near the line between the latter, upon a high rocky hill, is still to be found [in 1906] the remains of an old Indian fort, known from earliest times as the 'Queen's Fort,' and probably near the place where her deserted 'Quarters' were raided. The army that day destroyed one hundred and fifty wigwams, killed seven and captured nine Indians. In the meantime Captain Oliver had sent out 'five files,' i.e. thirty of his men, under Sergeant Peter Bennet, who, scouting abroad, killed two Indians, a man and a woman, and captured four more.

"Wednesday, December 15th, the army seems to have been held in parley most of the day by the pretended negotiations of 'Stone-wall' or 'Stone-layer,' John, an Indian who had lived much with the English, and had learned the trade of stone-mason, but was now hostile, and very serviceable to the Indians in many ways. Whether he was treacherous or not, the Indians were gathering and skulking about the English quarters while he was negotiating, and when he was safely away they began to pick off the English wherever they found an opportunity, and later lay in ambush behind a stone wall and fired upon several companies of the English sent out to bring in Major Appleton's company, quartered some miles away.

"They were quickly repulsed with the loss of one of their leaders, and seem to have gone towards the general rendezvous at the great fort, and on the way they assaulted and burned the garrison of Jireh, or 'Jerry' Bull at Pettisquamscot (Tower Hill, South Kingston), killing fifteen of those at the garrison, two only escaping."

The following, with minor changes, is taken from Samuel D. Drake's *Biography and History of the Indians of North America*, published in Boston in 1841.

"Magnus was squaw sachem of some part of the extensive country of the Narragansetts, and was known by several names at different and the same times, as Old Queen, Sunk Squaw, Quaiapen, and Matantuck. She married Mriksah, or Mexem, a son of Canonicus, and was sister to Ninigret. She had two sons, Scuttup and Quequaquenuct, called by the English Gideon, and a daughter named Quinemiquet. These two died young. Gideon was alive as late as 1661; Scuttup, and a sister also, in 1664. She was, in 1675, one of the six sachems of the whole Narragansett country.

"In the beginning of Philip's war, the English army, to cause the Narragansetts to fight for them, whom they had always abused and treated with contempt, since before the cutting off of Miantunnomah's head [Miantonomo, whom years earlier the English had allowed Uncas to murder, thus earning the hatred of the Narragansetts], marched into their country, but could not meet with a single sachem of the nation. The English fell in with a few of their people, who could not well secrete themselves, and who concluded a long treaty of mere verbosity, the import of which they could know but little, and doubtless cared less; for when the army left their country, they joined again in the war.

"The English caused four men to subscribe to their articles in the name, or in behalf of Quaiapen and the other chiefs, and took four others as hostages for their due fulfillment of those articles. Their names were Wobequob, Weowchim, Pewkes, and Wenew, who are said to have been 'near kinsmen and choice friends' to the sachems.

"We hear no more of Quaiapen until the next year, when herself and a large company of her men were discovered by Major [John] Talcott, on July 2 [1676], in Narragansett. The English scouts discovered them from a hill, having pitched their tents in a valley in the vicinity of a swamp, as was usually their custom. About three hundred of the English, mounted upon fleet horses, divided into two squadrons, and fell upon them before they were aware of their approach, and made a great slaughter.

"The Mohegans and Pequots came upon them in the center, while the horsemen beset them on each side, and thus prevented many from escaping into the swamp. When all were killed or taken within the encampment, Captain [Benjamin] Newbury, who commanded the horsemen, dismounted, and with his men rushed into the swamp, where, without resistance, they killed a hundred, and made many more prisoners.

"In all, they killed and took 171 [other contemporary historians put the figure closer to 240] in the swamp fight or rather massacre. Not an Englishman was hurt in the affair, and but one Mohegan killed, and one wounded, which we can hardly suppose was done by Quaiapen's people, as they made no resistance, but rather by themselves, in their fury mistaking one another. Ninety of the captives were put to death, among whom was Quaiapen. The swamp where this affair took place is near the present town of Warwick, in Rhode Island."

(Those readers desirous of a detailed description of the Queen's Fort, along with other pertinent facts, are directed to Appendix III.)

Mary Rowlandson

This narrative was penned by the gentlewoman herself, to be to her a memorandum of God's dealing with her, that she might never forget, but remember the same, and the several circumstances thereof, all the days of her life...

Reader, if thou gettest no good by such a declaration as this, the fault must needs be thine own. Read, therefore, peruse, ponder, and from hence lay by something from the experience of another against thine own turn comes...[from the Preface to the second edition of The Sovereignty & Goodness of God, Together With the Faithfulness of His Promises Displayed; Being a Narrative of the Captivity and Restoration of Mrs. Mary Rowlandson, *published in Cambridge, Massachusetts, in 1682]*

Mary Rowlandson has the distinction of being the first best-selling author in America. First published in Boston in 1682, *The Sovereignty and Goodness of God*, her account of her abduction and captivity during King Philip's War, saw two additional printings in Cambridge that same year, and another in London. Numerous editions appeared in the next century, and in the century after that; at least six editions saw print in the twentieth century. In the brief periods when it has been out of print, it has been readily available, in libraries and in used and antiquarian bookstores. Mary Rowlandson has the added distinction of having created, with her book, a distinct genre of popular American literature: the Captivity Narrative.

Despite the fact that she was English (the English kept records; the Indians did not) and highly literate (in an age when English women might be taught to read, but seldom to write), we know (as is the case with Awashonks, for example) few details of her life. Those details that we do know, especially regarding her early years, are somewhat sketchy.

Mary was born in Somerset, England, probably in South Petherton, sometime between 1635 and 1638. Her parents were John and Joane White; her mother's maiden name was West. Within a few years, possibly months, of her birth her family arrived in New England, settling first in the Salem area around 1638, and eventually moving, in 1653, to Lancaster (Nashaway), originally settled in 1643, and still very much a frontier town. Her mother died there the following year. Her father died, a wealthy man, in 1673, just two years before the war.

Mary had six siblings: Thomas, Joane, Elizabeth, Josiah, Sarah, and Hannah.

In 1656 she married Lancaster's young minister, Joseph Rowlandson. Joseph was born in England around 1631; his family settled in New England, in the Ipswich area, six or seven years later. He attended Harvard, graduating in 1652, and accepted the ministry in Lancaster in 1654. (He died in Wethersfield, Connecticut, in November, 1678.) The couple had four children. The first, named Mary after her mother, died around the age of three. The others (about whom more later) were Joseph, a second Mary, and Sarah.

⁂

On February 10, 1676, a mixed band of four hundred Indians led by the Narragansett sachem Quinnapin (whom we met earlier, in the chapter on Weetamoo) mounted an attack upon Lancaster. This, incidentally, was not the first time Indians had attacked that remote community. In August of the previous year a group of Nashaways, led by Monoco (also known as One-Eyed John, or Apequinash), had killed seven settlers there. The February 10th raid was more coordinated. Besides Quinnapin, the leaders of the attack included Monoco and Muttaump, sachem of Quabaug.

Nearly three weeks earlier, on January 24th, the Christian Indian spies James Quannapohit and Job Kattenanit had warned the English of an impending attack on Lancaster, but because of prejudice towards Indians in general, and lack of trust, the English had largely ignored the warnings. However, Joseph Rowlandson, Lancaster's minister and most prominent citizen, had taken the warnings seriously enough to travel to Boston to seek greater protection for the town. His brother-in-law, Lieutenant Henry Kerley, married to Mary's sister Elizabeth, accompanied him, as did a number of other influential community leaders.

On the night of February 9th, having traveled eighty miles on snowshoes from Menameset (New Braintree) all the way to Cambridge, Job Kattenanit had wakened Daniel Gookin (who at that time was superintendent of all the Praying Indian towns in Massachusetts) to once again advise that, in the morning, an army of four hundred Indians would attack Lancaster; as part of their plan, to prevent help from arriving or settlers from fleeing, they intended to destroy the bridge over the Nashua River that lead into town.

This time the English believed Job and dispatched messengers to alert Lancaster, as well as Concord and Marlborough.

Receiving the message, Samuel Wadsworth, captain in charge of the small company of soldiers stationed in Marlborough, hastened to Lancaster (a distance of ten miles) with about forty men. Meanwhile, eighty mounted troops were dispatched from Concord. Despite finding the bridge, as forewarned, partially destroyed, Wadsworth arrived in time to rescue survivors of the attack. (He himself, along with Captain Samuel Brocklebank, was killed a few months later at Green Hill, during the April 21, 1676, raid on Sudbury.)

The residents of Lancaster had sought refuge within six garrison houses: Joseph Rowlandson's, John Prescott's, Richard Wheeler's, Thomas Sawyer's, Nathaniel Joslin's, and Cyprian Stevens's. This latter garrison was near Rowlandson's but across the river; it was at this house that Wadsworth and his men arrived first.

All but the Rowlandson garrison were able to hold out against the enemy until help arrived. When, too late, the minister and his brother-in-law returned from Boston, they found the house destroyed, the occupants, their friends and loved ones, killed or taken captive. Among those taken were Mary Rowlandson and her three children.

"On the tenth of February, 1675, came the Indians with great numbers upon Lancaster." So begins Mary's account of her ordeal, (giving the date in the old style, in which the new year would not begin until March 25, the supposed birth date of the Virgin Mary). We do not know when she wrote her narrative: probably sometime in 1677, or possibly 1678. Nor are we absolutely certain of the year of her death. Some historians claim that she died before 1682, the year in which her book was first published; many of these same historians believe that her death occurred in 1678, the year her husband died, or shortly thereafter. Others claim to have found evidence that Mary survived her husband Joseph by nearly two decades, and that she married, in 1679, Captain Samuel Talcott; these historians give January 6, 1711, as the date of her death.

Why Mary Rowlandson wrote a detailed, often graphic, account of her ordeal is anyone's guess; many plausible motives have been suggested by scholars and historians. My guess is that she wrote it a means of catharsis, as a way of coming to terms with the hardships and horrors she witnessed and endured, and the grievous loss of so many loved ones--not least of which was that of her young daughter.

We can only be thankful that she did choose to write it all down, and to allow its publication, thereby giving future generations insights into aspects of the war (especially details of the daily lives of the Indians, her captors, while on the move, and the intimate sketches, however understandably biased, of, among others, Weetamoo and Philip) which we would otherwise lack.

In the brief excerpts from the book which follow, I have omitted the many references to the bible, and quotations from it, that Mary, a pious Puritan, wove into her narrative. In keeping with the theme of *Women in King Philip's War*, the excerpts are primarily, though by no means exclusively, those that pertain to Mary's interactions with other women.

Defense of Mr. Rowlandson's house.

"Their first coming was about sun rising. Hearing the noise of some guns, we looked out. Several houses were burning, and the smoke ascending to heaven. There were five persons taken in one house. The father [John Ball] and the mother and a sucking child they knocked on the head; the other two they took and carried away alive. There were two others who, being out of their garrison...were set upon. One was knocked on the head, the other escaped.

"Another there was who running along was shot and wounded and fell down. He begged of them his life, promising them money (as they told me), but they would not harken to him, but knocked him on the head, stripped him naked, and split open his bowels. Another, seeing many...Indians about his barn, ventured...out, but was quickly shot down. There were three others belonging to the same garrison [Richard Wheeler's] who were killed. The Indians, getting up upon the roof of the barn, had advantage to shoot down upon them over their fortification. Thus these murderous wretches went on, burning and destroying before them.

"At length they came and beset our own house, and quickly it was the dolefullest day that ever my eyes saw. The house stood upon the edge of a hill. Some of the Indians got behind the hill, others into the barn, and others behind anything that would shelter them, from all which places they shot against the house, so that the bullets seemed to fly like hail. And quickly they wounded one man among us, then another, and then a third. About two hours...they had been about the house before they prevailed to fire it (which they did with flax and hemp which they brought out of the barn--and there being no defense about the house, only two flankers [fortifications projecting from the side of the building] at two opposite corners, and one of them not finished). They fired it once, and one ventured out and quenched it; but they quickly fired it again, and that took...

"Some in our house were fighting for their lives, others wallowing in their blood, the house on fire over our heads, and the bloody heathen ready to knock us on the head if we stirred out...I took my children (and one of my sisters [Hannah Divoll], hers) to go forth and leave the house. But as soon as we came to the door and appeared, the Indians shot so thick that the bullets rattled against the house as if one had taken a handful of stones and threw them, so that we were fain to give back. We had six stout dogs belonging to our garrison, but none of them would stir, though another time if an Indian had come to the door, they were ready to fly upon him and tear him down.

"...Out we must go, the fire increasing and coming along behind us roaring and the Indians gaping before us with their guns, spears, and hatchets to devour us. No sooner were we out of the house, but my brother-in-law [Hannah's husband, John], being before wounded in defending the house, in or near the throat, fell down dead, whereat the Indians scornfully shouted and hallowed and were presently upon him, stripping off his clothes. The bullets flying thick, one went through my side, and the same (as would seem) through the bowels and hand of my dear child [Sarah] in my arms. One of my elder sister [Elizabeth]'s children (named William) had then his leg broken--which the Indians perceiving, they knocked him on the head.

"Thus were we butchered by those merciless heathen, standing amazed, with the blood running down to our heels. My elder sister being yet in the house and seeing those woeful sights--the infidels haling mothers one way and children another, and some wallowing in their blood, and her elder son [Henry, Jr.] telling her that William was dead and myself wounded--she said, *Lord, let me die with them.* Which was no sooner said, but she was struck with a bullet and fell down dead over the threshold...

"The Indians laid hold of us, pulling me one way and the children another...Of thirty-seven persons who were in this one house, none escaped either present death or a bitter captivity, save only one...There were twelve killed--some shot, some stabbed with their spears, some knocked down with their hatchets...There was one who was chopped into the head with a hatchet and stripped naked, and yet was crawling up and down...There were twenty-four of us taken alive and carried captive."

The one who escaped the garrison was Ephraim Roper. His wife, Priscilla, and their three-year-old daughter, also named Priscilla, were killed. Roper was also one of the few to survive the debacle at Turner's Falls on May 19th, in which the English, led by Captain Turner, first massacred a number of sleeping Indians, and then were themselves slaughtered in large number. Ironically, Roper was killed (along with his wife and daughter) on September 11, 1697, when Lancaster was again attacked, during King William's War.

The grief and despair experienced by Lieutenant Henry Kerley, chief military officer of Lancaster, upon his return with Joseph Rowlandson from Boston can only be imagined: his wife, Elizabeth, dead, as well as his sons William and Joseph. The other five children, Henry, Jr., Elizabeth, Hannah, Mary, and Martha, were all taken captive. What happened to them after that is not known.

The fate of Hannah, Mary's younger sister, was likewise tragic. Her husband, John Divoll, whom she married in 1663, and who held the rank of ensign, was killed in the attack, as was their son Josiah, aged seven. Hannah was taken captive, as were their three other children, John, Jr., Hannah, and William. Hannah and her son William were eventually ransomed; the fate of John, Jr. and little Hannah is not known.

Having described the attack and her capture, Mrs. Rowlandson went on: "That I may the better declare what happened to me during that grievous captivity, I shall particularly speak of the several removes we had up and down the wilderness." In The First Remove, she tells us that on the first night the Indians camped on a hill about a mile from town [George Hill, named after an Indian who once lived there], and feasted on "horses, cattle, sheep, swine, calves, lambs, roasting pigs, and fowls (which they had plundered...)." She tells how she reflected on her losses and concern for her husband and children. "There remained nothing to me but one poor, wounded babe [Sarah, about six years old], and it seemed at present worse than death that it was in such a pitiful condition, bespeaking compassion, and I had no refreshing for it, nor suitable things to revive it."

In The Second Remove she tells us, "One of the Indians carried my poor wounded babe upon a horse. It went moaning all along, I shall die, I shall die. I went on foot after it, with sorrow that cannot be expressed. At length I took it off the horse and carried it in my arms till my strength failed, and I fell down with it. Then they set me upon a horse with my wounded child in my lap, and there being no furniture upon the horse's back. As we were going down a steep hill, we both fell over the horse's head--at which they like inhuman creatures laughed and rejoiced to see it, though I thought we should there have ended our days, as overcome with so many difficulties..."

"After this it quickly began to snow, and when night came on they stopped. And now I must sit in the snow (by a little fire, and a few boughs behind me) with my sick child in my lap."

She begins The Third Remove: "The morning being come, they prepared to go on their way." She describes the hardships of the next several days, the cold, the lack of food, "there being not the least crumb of refreshing that came within either of our mouths from Wednesday to Saturday, except only a little cold water," and the great suffering of her wounded daughter. They arrive at Wenimesset, an Indian town north of Brookfield. "Thus nine days I sat upon my knees with my babe in my lap, till my flesh was raw...About two hours in the night, my sweet babe like a lamb departed this life.

"In the morning, when they understood that my child was dead, they sent for me home to my master's [Quinnapin's] wigwam." (She explains that Quinnapin had bought her from the Narragansett who "took me when first I came out of the garrison.") The Indians bury Sarah upon a hill and then show her the grave.

"God having taken away this dear child, I went to see my daughter Mary, who was at this same Indian town, at a wigwam not very far off, though we had little liberty or opportunity to see one another. She was about ten years old, and taken from the door at first by a Praying Indian, and afterwards sold for a gun. When I came in sight, she would fall a weeping; at which they were provoked and would not let me come near her...

"As I was going up and down mourning and lamenting my condition, my son came to me and asked how I did. I had not seen him before, since the destruction of the town... At this time, there were some forces of the Indians gathered out of our company and some also from them (amongst whom was my son's master) to go to assault and burn Medfield [February 26]. In this time of the absence of his master, his dame brought him to see me."

She describes the return of the victorious Indians from Medfield the following day: "Oh the hideous insulting and

69

triumphing that there was over some Englishmen's scalps." She goes on to say, "I cannot but take notice of the wonderful mercy of God to me in those afflictions, in sending me a Bible. One of the Indians that came from the Medfield fight and had brought some plunder came to me and asked me if I would have a Bible; he had got one in his basket." (Mary seems to overlook the fact that, in sending her a bible, God deprived someone else of his or hers, possibly along with that person's life.)

She tells us that, of the nine other English captives with her in Wenimesset, eight were children, and the ninth a woman named Ann Joslin, who was "very big with child and had but one week to reckon, and another child in her arms, two years old." Ann was twenty-six years old; her husband, Abraham, one of the defenders of the Rowlandson garrison, had been killed in the attack.

❧

The plight of Ann Joslin calls to mind that of other female English captives in King Philip's War, as well as in later conflicts. Adult male captives, if they were not being held for ransom, were sometimes, indeed frequently, tortured to death. Women captives of the Algonquins were seldom mistreated, unless, because of physical incapacity, they were unable to keep up with the group, in which case they were "knocked on the head." The Algonquins did not sexually abuse women prisoners, a fact which seems to have amazed the English, who, perhaps, were themselves less considerate of their female Indian captives.

(Although the English did not torture prisoners, they sometimes allowed their Indian allies to do so. And Captain Samuel Moseley, noted for his hatred of Indians, frequently mistreated prisoners, of either sex. On one occasion he casually mentioned, in a letter to the governor of Massachusetts, having had a squaw torn to death by dogs.)

William Hubbard, in *A Narrative of the Troubles with the Indians in New-England*, published in Boston in 1677, records that in early March Goodwife Joslin, being unable to travel--at a time when the Indians were being pursued by an army led by Major Thomas Savage of Boston--was killed by her captors, along with her newborn child.

❧

Mary begins The Fourth Remove: "And now I must part with that little company that I had. Here I parted from my daughter Mary (whom I never saw again till I saw her in Dorchester, returned from captivity) and from four little cousins and neighbors, some of which I never saw afterward--the Lord only knows the end of them...We traveled about half a day or a little more and came to a desolate place in the wilderness, where there were no wigwams or inhabitants before. We came about the middle of the afternoon to this place, cold and wet and snowy and hungry and weary, and no refreshing (for man) but the cold ground to sit on." Her only consolation was her bible, "a sweet cordial to me when I was ready to faint."

And The Fifth Remove: "The occasion...of their moving at this time was the English army [the combined forces of Major Savage and a Connecticut contingent led by Major Robert Treat]...For they went as if they had gone for their lives for some considerable way, and then they made a stop and chose out some of their stoutest men, and sent them back to hold the English army in play whilst the rest escaped. And then...they marched on furiously, with their old and their young. Some carried their old decrepit mothers; some carried one, and some another. Four of them carried a great Indian upon a bier, but, going through a thick wood with him, they were hindered and could make no haste; whereupon they took him upon their backs and carried him, one at a time, till we came to Bacquag [Miller's] River [near Orange or Athol]...

"In this travel because of my wound, I was somewhat favored in my load: I carried only my knitting-work and two quarts of parched meal. Being very faint, I asked my mistress [Weetamoo] to give me one spoonful of the meal, but she would not give me the taste. They quickly fell to cutting dry trees to make rafts to carry them over the river, and soon my turn came...By the advantage of some brush which they had laid upon the raft to sit, I did not wet my foot...

"A certain number of us got over the river that night, but it was the night after the Sabbath [March 5th] before all the company was got over. On the Saturday, they boiled an old horse's leg...and so we drank of the broth as soon as they thought it was ready, and when it was almost gone, they filled it up again.

"The first week of my being among them I hardly ate anything. The second week I found my stomach grow very faint for want of something, and yet 'twas very hard to get down their filthy trash. But the third week (though I could think how formerly my stomach would turn against this or that, and I could starve and die before I could eat such things, yet) they were pleasant and savory to my taste. I was at this time knitting a pair of white cotton stockings for my mistress..."

Mary complains about being compelled by the Indians to work on the Sabbath, and continues: "I cannot but take notice of the strange providence of God in preserving the heathen. They were many hundreds, old and young, some sick and some lame; many had papooses at their backs. The greatest number at this time with us were squaws, and they traveled with all they had, bag and baggage. And yet they got over the river; and on Monday they set their wigwams on fire, and away they went. On that very day came the English army after them to this river and saw the smoke of their wigwams, and yet this river put a stop to them."

In The Sixth Remove she describes how, "mourning and lamenting," she traveled into "the vast and howling wilderness." And in The Seventh: "After a restless and hungry night, we had a wearisome time of it...The swamp by which we lay was, as it were, a deep dungeon, and an exceeding high and steep hill before it. Before I got to the top...I thought my heart and legs and all would have broken and failed me...

"That day, a little after noon, we came to Squakheag [Northfield], where the Indians quickly spread themselves over the deserted English fields, gleaning what they could find. Some picked up ears of wheat that were crickled down; some found ears of Indian corn; some found ground nuts and others sheaves of wheat that were frozen together in the shock...Myself got two ears of Indian corn, and whilst I did but turn my back, one of them was stolen from me.

"There came an Indian...with a basket of horse liver. I asked him to give me a piece...which he did, and I laid it on the coals to roast; but before it was half ready, they got half of it away from me, so that I was fain to take the rest and eat it as it was, with the blood around my mouth. And yet a savory bit it was to me...That night we had a mess of wheat for our supper."

In The Eighth Remove they "traveled on till night, and in the morning we must go over the river to [King] Philip's crew. When I was in the canoe I could not but be amazed at the numerous crew of pagans that were on the bank on the other side. When I came ashore, they gathered all about me." Mary

Captivity of Mrs. Rowlandson.

73

loses heart, and for the first time since her capture begins to weep. "Then came one of them and gave me two spoonsful of meal (to comfort me), and another gave me half a pint of peas, which was more worth than many bushels at another time.

"Then I went to see King Philip; he bade me come in and sit down, and asked me whether I would smoke...But this no way suited me. For though I had formerly used tobacco, yet I had left it ever since I was first taken. It seems to be a bait the devil lays to make men lose their precious time...Surely, there are many who may be better employed than to lie sucking a stinking tobacco pipe...

"During my abode in this place, Philip spoke to me to make a shirt for his boy--which I did, for which he gave me a shilling. I offered the money to my master, but he bade me keep it, and with it I bought a piece of horse flesh. Afterwards he asked me to make a cap for his boy, for which he invited me to dinner. I went, and he gave me a pancake about as big as two fingers; it was made of parched wheat, beaten and fried in bear's grease, but I thought I never tasted pleasanter meat in my life.

"There was a squaw who spoke to me to make a shirt for her sannup [husband], for which she gave me a piece of bear. Another asked me to knit a pair of stockings, for which she gave me a quart of peas. I boiled my peas and bear together and invited my master and mistress to dinner; but the proud gossip, because I served them both in one dish, would eat nothing, except one bit that he gave her upon the point of his knife."

She finds her son lying on the ground, praying, and expresses the wish that he will remember his piety "now he is returned to safety" (referring to the fact that he was eventually ransomed for seven pounds and released in New Hampshire). Because of the bright sun and smoke from the wigwams she has trouble seeing. "Mary Thurston of Medfield, who, seeing how it was with me, lent me a hat to wear; but as soon as I was gone, the squaw (who owned that Mary Thurston) came running after me and got it away again. Here there was a squaw who gave me one spoonful of meal. I put it in my pocket to keep it safe; yet notwithstanding somebody stole it, but put five Indian corns in the room of it--which corns were the greatest provision I had in my travel for one day.

"The Indians returning from Northampton brought with them some horses and sheep and other things which they had taken. I desired them that they would carry me to Albany upon one of those horses and sell me for powder, for so they had sometimes discoursed. I was utterly hopeless of getting home on foot...I could hardly bear to think of the many weary steps I had taken to come to this place."

And so to The Ninth Remove: "But instead of going either to Albany or homeward, we must go five miles up the river and go over it. Here we abode for a while [most likely southern New Hampshire]. Here there lived a sorry Indian who spoke to me to make him a shirt; when I had done it, he would pay me nothing. But he living by the river side, where I often went to fetch water, I would often be putting him in mind and calling for my pay. At last he told me if I would make him another shirt, for a papoose not yet born, he would give me a knife, which he did...I carried the knife in, and my master asked me to give it to him, and I was not a little glad that I had anything that they would accept and be pleased with.

"When we were at this place, my master's maid came home; she had gone three weeks into the Narragansett country to fetch corn where they had stored some in the ground. She brought home about a peck and a half of corn. This was about the time that their great captain [Canonchet] was killed." (Canonchet was captured on April 2, and executed the following day.)

Mary learns that her son is about a mile from her, and with permission goes to visit him. When she returns she is "fain to go and look for something to satisfy my hunger, and going among the wigwams I went into one and there found a squaw who showed herself very kind to me and gave me a piece of bear. I put it into my pocket and came home, but could not find an opportunity to broil it, for fear they would get it from me, and there it lay all that day and night in my stinking pocket.

"In the morning I went again to the same squaw, who had a kettle of ground-nuts boiling. I asked her to let me boil my piece of bear in her kettle, which she did and gave me some ground-nuts to eat with it; and I cannot but think how pleasant it was to me. I have sometime seen bear baked very handsomely amongst the English, and some like it, but the thoughts that it was bear made me tremble; but now that was savory to me that one would think was enough to turn the stomach of a brute creature.

"One bitter cold night I could find no room to sit down before the fire. I went out and could not tell what to do, but I went into another wigwam, where they were also sitting round the fire. But the squaw laid a skin for me and bade me sit down, and gave me some ground-nuts and bade me come again, and told me they would buy me if they were able; and yet these were strangers to me that I never knew before."

In The Tenth Remove they travel less than a mile. Here Mary is met with unkindness: an Indian who, when she seeks warmth, "kicked me all along. I went home and found venison roasting that night, but they would not give me one bit of it. Sometimes I met with favor and sometimes with nothing but frowns." In The Eleventh Remove they "passed over tiresome and wearisome hills. One hill was so steep that I was fain to creep up upon my knees and to hold by the twigs and bushes to keep myself from falling backwards."

In The Twelfth Remove Mary experiences further difficulties with Weetamoo, who, finding her reading her bible, "snatched it hastily out of my hand and threw it out of doors. I ran out and catched it up, and put it into my pocket and never let her see it afterward." Mary complains that the load she is carrying is too heavy, "whereupon she gave me a slap in the face..."

She continues to suffer from hunger and cold. "I went to one wigwam, and they told me they had no room. Then I went to another, and they said the same. At last an old Indian bade me come to him, and his squaw gave me some ground-nuts; she gave me also something to lay under my head, and a good fire we had." But the next morning as they travel near the Connecticut River, "I went with a great load at my back. I told them the skin was off my back, but I had no other comforting answer from them than this: that it would be no matter if my head were off too."

Things don't get much better for Mary in The Thirteenth Remove: "I must go with them five or six miles down the river into a mighty thicket of brush, where we abode almost a fortnight [still in New Hampshire]. Here one asked me to make a shirt for her papoose, for which she gave me a mess of broth which was thickened with meal made of the bark of a tree; and to make it better she had put into it about a handful of peas and a few roasted ground-nuts...

"In this place on a cold night, as I lay by the fire, I removed a stick which kept the heat from me; a squaw moved it down again, at which I looked up, and she threw a handful of ashes in my eyes. I thought I should have been quite blinded and have never seen more; but lying down the water ran out of my eyes and carried the dirt with it, that by morning I recovered my sight again."

Mary's hopes of being either rescued or ransomed fade with each passing day; she despairs of ever being reunited with her husband and her two surviving children. "About this time they came yelping from Hadley, having there killed three Englishmen and brought one captive..." The captive was Thomas Reed, who was taken on April 1st. He tells Mary that he has seen her husband, who was well, "but very melancholy." (Reed later escaped, and on May 18 led Captain William Turner and his army of one hundred and fifty men and boys from Hatfield to the Indian encampment at Peskeompskut--the Upper Falls in Montague.)

"As I was sitting once in the wigwam here, Philip's maid came in with the child in her arms and asked me to give her a piece of my apron to make a flap for it; I told her I would not. Then my mistress bade me give it, but still I said no. The maid told me if I would not give her a piece, she would tear a piece of it; I told her I would tear her coat then. With that, my mistress rises up and takes a stick big enough to have killed me and struck at me with it, but I stepped out, and she struck the stick into the mat of the wigwam. But while she was pulling it out, I ran to the maid and gave her all my apron, and so that storm was over."

Mary tries to help another English captive, a seventeen-year-old youth, John Gilbert, from Springfield, who though seriously ill has been "turned out of the wigwam, and with him an Indian papoose, almost dead (whose parents had been killed), in a bitter cold day, without fire or clothes; the young man himself had nothing on but his shirt and waistcoat." With "much ado" she is able to get Gilbert to a fire.

Gilbert's master's daughter demands to know what Mary has done with him. "For her satisfaction I went along with her and brought her to him; but before I got home again it was noised about that I was running away...as soon as I came in, they began to rant and domineer, asking me where I had been and what I had been doing, and saying they would knock me on the head...they told me I lied, and taking up a hatchet, they came to me and said they would knock me down if I stirred out again."

As punishment Mary is confined to the wigwam, but having knitted a pair of stockings for an Indian, she is allowed by Weetamoo to go outside with him; he gives her some roasted ground-nuts. Out of sight of Weetamoo, she reads her bible. She again meets her son, who is very hungry; she suggests that he "go into the wigwams...to see if he could get anything among them. Which he did, and (it seems) tarried a little too long, for his master was angry with him and beat him, and then sold him. Then he came running to tell me he had a new master and that he had given him some ground-nuts already. Then I went along with him to his new master who told me he loved him, and he should not want. So his master carried him away, and I never saw him afterward till I saw him at Piscataqua in Portsmouth."

And so to The Fourteenth Remove: "Now we must pack up and be gone from this thicket, bending our course toward the [Massachusetts] Bay towns--I having nothing to eat by the way this day but a few crumbs of cake that an Indian gave my girl the same day we were taken. She gave it me, and I put it into my pocket; there it lay till it was so moldy (for want of good baking) that one could not tell what it was made of. It fell all to crumbs and grew so dry and hard that it was like little flints; and this refreshed me many times when I was ready to faint...

"As we went along, they killed a deer with a young in her; they gave me a piece of the fawn, and it was so young and tender that one might eat the bones as well as the flesh, and yet I thought it was very good. When night came on, we sat down; it rained, but they quickly got up a bark wigwam, where I lay dry that night. I looked out in the morning, and many of them had lain in the rain all night...

"In the morning, they took the blood of the deer and put it into the paunch and so boiled it; I could eat nothing of that, though they ate it sweetly. And yet they were so nice [squeamish] in other things that, when I had fetched water and had put the dish I dipped the water with into the kettle of water which I brought, they would say they would knock me down; for they said it was a sluttish trick."

In her account of The Fifteenth Remove, Mary reflects on her near starvation. "And after I was thoroughly hungry, I was never again satisfied. For though sometimes it fell out that I got enough and did eat until I could eat no more, yet I was as unsatisfied as when I began." Her religious faith, however, continues to sustain her. And the great Wheel of Fortune begins a slow turn.

"We began this remove [The Sixteenth] with wading over Baquaug river. The water was up to the knees, and the stream very swift and so cold that I thought it would have cut me in sunder. I was so weak and feeble that I reeled as I went along and thought there I must end my days...The Indians stood laughing to see me staggering along...

"Quickly there came up to us an Indian who informed them that I must go to Wachusett to my master, for there was a letter come from the Council to the sagamores about redeeming the captives...My heart was so heavy before that I could scarcely speak or go in the path, and yet now so light that I could run."

The letter from the Council was carried by Nepanet, a Christian Indian, also known as Tom Dublet. On March 31, 1676, he was released from internment on Deer Island and sent to Wachusett as an emissary to negotiate for the return of captives. Samuel D. Drake, in *Biography and History of the Indians of North America*, published in Boston in 1841, fills in the details:

"Tom Nepanet was fixed upon as plenipotentiary in this business. And, although unjustly suffering with many of his brethren upon a bleak island in Boston Harbor, consented, at the imminent risk of his life, to proceed to meet the Indians in the western wilderness, in the service, and for the benefit, of those who had caused his sufferings.

"Nepanet set out, April 12th, 1676, to make overtures to the enemy for the release of prisoners, especially the family of Mr. Rowlandson, which was taken at Lancaster. He soon returned with a written answer from the enemy, saying, 'We no give answer by this one man, but if you like my answer send one more besides this one Tom Napanet, and send with all true heart and with your mind by two men; because you know and we know your heart great sorrowful with crying for your lost many many hundred man and all your house and all your land and woman child and cattle as all your thing that you have lost.'

"At the same time, and I conclude in the same letter, they wrote a few words to others as follows: 'Mr. Rowlandson, your wife and all your child is well but one die. Your sister is well and her 3 child.--John Kittell, your wife and all your child is all well, and all them prisoners taken at Nashua is all well.--

"'Mr. Rowlandson, see your loving sister his hand. Hannah. And old Kettel wife his hand X

"'Brother Rowlandson, pray send three pound of Tobacco for me, if you can my loving husband pray send three pound of tobacco for me.

"'This writing by your enemies--Samuel Uskattuhgum and Gunrashit, two Indian sagamores.'"

(The John Kettle--variously spelled--addressed in the letter may actually have been killed in the attack on Lancaster. George M. Bodge, in *Soldiers in King Philip's War*, published in 1906, citing H. S. Nourse's "Early Records of Lancaster" as his source, gives, among the names of those killed, John Kettle, aged 36; John Kettle, Jr.; and Joseph Kettle, son of John, aged ten.)

In The Seventeenth Remove, Mary starts off in good spirits, but her strength soon flags. "At night we came to an Indian town, and the Indians sat down by a wigwam discoursing, but I was almost spent and could scarce speak. I laid down my load and went into the wigwam, and there sat an Indian boiling of horse's feet (they being wont to eat the flesh first, and when the feet were old and dried and they had nothing else they would cut off the feet and use them).

"I asked him to give me a little of his broth or water they were boiling in; he took a dish and gave me one spoonful of samp [coarse hominy], and bid me take as much of the broth as I would. Then I put some of the hot water to the samp and drank it up, and my spirit came again. He gave me also a piece of the ruffe [rough] or ridding of the small guts, and I broiled it on the coals..."

On The Eighteenth Remove: "We took up our packs, and along we went. But a wearisome day I had of it. As we went along, I saw an Englishman stripped naked and lying dead upon the ground, but knew not who it was. Then we came to another Indian town, where we stayed all night. In this town there were four English children, captives, and one of them my own sister's [either Hannah Divoll's or Elizabeth Kerley's]. I went to see how she did, and she was well, considering her captive-condition. I would have tarried that night with her, but they that owned her would not suffer it.

"Then I went to another wigwam, where they were boiling corn and beans, which was a lovely sight to see; but I could not get a taste thereof. Then I went into another wigwam, where there were two of the English children; the squaw was boiling horse's feet. Then she cut me off a little piece and gave one of the children a piece also. Being very hungry, I had quickly eaten up mine, but the child could not bit it--it so tough and sinewy--but lay sucking, gnawing, chewing, and slobbering of it in the mouth and hand; then I took it of the child and ate it myself, and savory it was to my taste...

"Then I went home to my mistress's wigwam, and they told me I disgraced my master with begging and, if I did so any more, they would knock me in the head; I told them they had as good knock me on the head as starve me to death."

Fortune's Wheel, however, keeps turning. The Nineteenth Remove, which begins in mid April and lasts for nine long days, brings Mary ever closer to freedom.

"They said, when we went out, that we must travel to Wachusett this day. But a bitter weary day I had of it, traveling now three days together, without resting any day between. At last, after many weary steps, I saw Wachusett hills, but many miles off. Then we came to a great swamp, through which we traveled up to the knees in mud and water--which was heavy going for one tired before. Being almost spent, I thought I should have sunk down at last and never get out...Going along, having indeed my life, but little spirit, Philip (who was in the company) came up and took me by the hand, and said, *two weeks more and you shall be mistress again*. I asked him if he spoke true. He answered, *Yes, and quickly you shall come to your master again*--who had been gone from us three weeks.

"After many weary steps, we came to Wachusett, where he was; and glad I was to see him. He asked me when I washed me. I told him not this month; then he fetched me some water himself and bid me wash, and gave me the glass to see how I looked and bade his squaw [Onux] give me something to eat. So she gave me a mess of beans and meat, and a little groundnut cake. I was wonderfully revived with this favor showed me...

"My master had three squaws, living sometimes with one and sometimes with another--one, this old squaw at whose wigwam I was, and with whom my master had been those three weeks. Another was Weetamoo, with whom I had lived and served all this while. A severe and proud dame she was, bestowing every day in dressing herself near as much time as any of the gentry of the land--powdering her hair and painting her face, going with her necklaces, with jewels in her ears and bracelets upon her hands. When she had dressed herself, her work was to make girdles of wampum and beads. The third squaw was a younger one, by whom he had two papooses.

"By that time I was refreshed by the old squaw with whom my master was, Weetamoo's maid came to call me home, at which I fell a-weeping; then the old squaw told me, to encourage me, that if I wanted victuals, I should come to her, and that I should lie there in her wigwam. Then I went with the maid and quickly came again and lodged there. The squaw laid a mat under me and a good rug over me, the first time I had any such kindness showed me. I understood that Weetamoo thought that, if she should let me go and serve with the old squaw, she would be in danger to lose not only my service, but the redemption pay also.

"...Then came an Indian and asked me to knit him three pair of stockings, for which I had a hat and a silk handkerchief. Then another asked me to make her a shirt, for which she gave me an apron.

"Then came Tom and Peter with the second letter from the Council about the captives. [Tataiquinea, also known as Peter Conway, was, like Nepanet, a Christian Indian from Nashoba released from Deer Island.] Though they were Indians, I got them by the hand and burst out into tears; my heart was so full that I could not speak to them. But, recovering myself,

I asked them how my husband did, and all my friends and acquaintances. They said they were well, but very melancholy. They brought me two biscuits and a pound of tobacco. The tobacco I quickly gave away; when it was all gone, one asked me to give him a pipe of tobacco. I told him it was all gone; then began he to rant and threaten. I told him when my husband came I would give him some. *Hang him, Rogue* (says he), *I will knock out his brains if he comes here.* And then again in the same breath they would say that if there should come a hundred without guns, they would do them no hurt...

"When the letter was come, the sagamores met to consult about the captives and called me to them to inquire how much my husband would give to redeem me...Now knowing that all we had was destroyed by the Indians, I was in a great strait. I thought if I should speak of but a little, it would be slighted and hinder the matter; if of a great sum, I knew not where it would be procured. Yet at a venture I said *Twenty pounds*, yet desired them to take less; but they would not hear of that, but sent that message to Boston...It was a Praying Indian that wrote that letter for them."

The Praying Indian whom Mary refers to is James the Printer, also known as Wowaus. A Nipmuck, he was born in 1643 in the Praying Indian town of Hassanamesitt (present-day Grafton), and educated in Cambridge, where he worked as a printer for sixteen years. On August 30, 1675, he was one of fifteen Christian Indians forcibly seized by Captain Moseley without provocation and brutally marched (with a rope around his neck) to Boston, where he spent time in jail and was put on trial, and acquitted. In November he rejoined the Nipmucks when they raided Hassanemesit. He served as scribe for Mary's captors in their negotiations.

Toward the end of the war he surrendered (bringing with him, as instructed, the heads of two enemy Indians), was granted immunity, and resumed work as a printer. Ironically, in 1682 he set the type for Mary's captivity narrative. (He assisted John Eliot in setting type for the second edition of the Indian bible, completed in 1686. He continued as apprentice until 1709. He died in 1728.)

The letter he wrote reads as follows: "The Indians, Tom Nepennomp and Peter Tatatiquinea hath brought us letter from you about the English Captives, especially for Mrs. Rolanson; the answer is I am sorrow that I have don much wrong to you, for when we began quarrel at first with Plimouth men I did not think that you should have so much trouble as now is: therefore I am willing to hear your desire about the Captives. Therefore we desire you to send Mr. Rolanson and goodman Kettel: (for their wives) and these Indians Tom and Peter to redeem their wives, they shall come and go very safely: Whereupon we ask Mrs. Rolanson, how much your husband willing to give for you she gave an answer 20 pound in goods but John Kittels wife could not tell. And the rest captives may be spoken hereafter."

Mary spends the next two pages of her book complaining about the hypocrisy of the Praying Indians--overlooking the fact that most of the Christian Indians who eventually joined the enemy, such as James the Printer, did so only after extreme provocation on the part of the bigoted English. She also overlooks the fact that it was the innocent Christian Indians Nepanet and Tataiquinea (Tom and Peter), who, after having been placed into what amounted to a concentration camp on Deer Island, where they suffered greatly, volunteered to undertake the dangerous mission of negotiating for her release.

Resuming her narrative, she tells us that "When my master came home, he came to me and bid me make a shirt for his papoose...About that time there came an Indian to me and bid me come to his wigwam at night, and he would give me some pork and ground-nuts. Which I did, and as I was eating another Indian said to me, *he seems to be your good friend, but he killed two Englishmen at Sudbury* [which about five hundred Indians led by Muttaump attacked on April 21st], *and there lie their clothes behind you.*

"I looked behind me, and there I saw bloody clothes, with bullet holes in them; yet the Lord suffered not this wretch to do me any hurt. Yea, instead of that, he many times refreshed me; five or six times did he and his squaw refresh my feeble carcass. If I went to their wigwam at any time, they would always give me something, and yet they were strangers that I never saw before. Another squaw gave me a piece of fresh pork and a little salt with it, and lent me her frying pan to fry it in; and I cannot but remember what a sweet, pleasant, and delightful relish that bit had to me, to this day. So little do we prize common mercies when we have them to the full."

And so to The Twentieth, and final, Remove: "It was their usual manner to remove when they had done any mischief, lest they should be found out, and so they did at this time. We went about three or four miles, and there they built a great wigwam, big enough to hold a hundred Indians, which they did in preparation to a great day of dancing. They would say amongst themselves that the Governor [John Leverett] would be so angry for his loss at Sudbury that he would send no more about the captives--which made me grieve and tremble.

"My sister [Hannah Divoll], being not far from the place where we now were and hearing that I was here, desired her master to let her come and see me, and he was willing to it and would go with her; but she, being ready before him, told him she would be before and was come within a mile or two of the place. Then he overtook her and began to rant as if he had been mad, and made her go back again in the rain, so that I never saw her till I saw her in Charlestown. But the Lord requited many of their ill-doings, for this Indian, her master, was hanged afterward at Boston.

"The Indians now began to come from all quarters against their merry dancing-day. Amongst some of them came one Goodwife Kettle. I told her my heart was so heavy that it was ready to break. *So is mine too,* said she, but yet said, *I hope we shall hear some good news shortly.* [Elizabeth Kettle was taken from the Rowlandson garrison along with her daughter Sarah, aged fourteen, her son Jonathan, aged five, and another child, age and name unknown. Mrs. Kettle was eventually ransomed.

Sarah escaped. The fate of the other two children is unknown.]

"I could hear how earnestly my sister desired to see me, and I as earnestly desired to see her; and yet neither of us could get an opportunity. My daughter was also now but about a mile off, and I had not seen her in nine or ten weeks, as I had not seen my sister since our first taking…"

In the midst of Mary's despondency the good news which Goodwife Kettle hoped for arrives: "On a Sabbath day [April 30th], the sun being about an hour high in the afternoon, came Mr. John Hoar…together with…Tom and Peter, with the third letter from the Council."

John Hoar was born in England around 1622. He lived in Scituate in the 1640's, then moved to Concord, where he was commissioned by the court to supervise the Christian Indians there. Against his protests, fifty-eight Indians were forcibly removed by Captain Moseley--the notorious Indian-hater--to Boston, where they were mistreated. Outspoken, and not at all sympathetic toward the Puritans, Hoar was disbarred by the Massachusetts General Court, and incurred numerous fines, but remained defiant to the end. He died in 1704.

Mary devotes roughly two pages relating various incidents involving Hoar's arrival. Bodge, in *Soldiers in King Philip's War*, tells us that "The place where Mr. Hoar met the Sachems is well identified, being marked by a large rock called 'Redemption Rock,' a noble landmark near the ancient Indian trail, between Lancaster and Mount Wachusett, and in the present town of Princeton, on the easterly side of a beautiful valley, across which, in the distance, towers Mount Wachusett.

"The locality is known as 'Everettville,' from the name of an ancient family who have lived here for generations. In 1880, Hon. Geo. F. Hoar, of Worcester, a lineal descendant of the chief actor in this transaction, for the English, purchased the land containing the site, and set it apart for memorial purposes, and caused the following inscription to be placed upon the face of the rock:

UPON THIS ROCK MAY 2ND 1676
WAS MADE THE AGREEMENT FOR THE RANSOM
OF MRS. MARY ROWLANDSON OF LANCASTER
BETWEEN THE INDIANS AND JOHN HOAR
OF CONCORD.
KING PHILIP WAS WITH THE INDIANS BUT
REFUSED HIS CONSENT.

Hoar, Mary tells us, has brought provisions, and on the day after his arrival invites the sagamores to dinner. "Mr. Hoar called them betime to dinner, but they ate very little, they being so busy in dressing themselves and getting ready for the dance, which was carried on by eight of them, four men and four squaws, my master and mistress being two. [Quinnapin]…was dressed in his Holland shirt, with great laces sewed at the tail of it; he had his silver buttons, his white stockings. His garters were hung round with shillings, and he had girdles of wampum upon his head and shoulders.

"…[Weetamoo] had a kersey coat covered with girdles of wampum from the loins upward. Her arms from her elbows to her hands were covered with bracelets; there were handfuls of necklaces about her neck and several sorts of jewels in her ears. She had fine red stockings and white shoes, her hair powdered and her face painted red, that was always before black. And all the dancers were after the same manner. There were two others singing and knocking on a kettle for their music. They kept hopping up and down one after another, with a kettle of water in the midst standing warm upon some embers, to drink when they were dry. They held on till it was almost night, throwing out wampum to the standersby.

"At night I asked them again if I should go home. They all as one said no, except my husband would come for me. When we were lain down, my master went out of the wigwam and by and by sent in…James the Printer, who told Mr. Hoar that my master would let me go home tomorrow if he would let him have one pint of liquors. Then Mr. Hoar called his own Indians, Tom and Peter, and bid them all go and see whether he would promise it before them three; and, if he would, he should have it--which he did, and had it.

"Then Philip, smelling the business, called me to him and asked me what I would give him to tell me some good news and to speak a good word for me, that I might go home tomorrow. I told him I could not tell what to give him--I would anything I had--and asked him what he would have. He said two coats and twenty shillings in money, and half a bushel of seed-corn and some tobacco. I thanked him for his love, but I knew the good news as well as that crafty fox.

"My master, after he had had his drink, quickly came ranting into the wigwam again, and called for Mr. Hoar, drinking to him and saying he was a good man; and then again he would say, *Hang him, Rogue*. Being almost drunk, he would drink to him and yet presently say he should be hanged. Then he called for me; I trembled to hear him, yet I was fain to go to him. And he drank to me, showing no incivility. He was the first Indian I saw drunk all the while that I was amongst them. At last his squaw ran out and he after her, round the wigwam, with his money jingling at his knees; but she escaped him. But, having an old squaw, he ran to her, and so through the Lord's mercy we were no more troubled with him that night.

"…On Tuesday morning [May 2] they called their General Court (as they styled it) to consult and determine whether I should go home or no; and they all as one man did seemingly consent to it, that I should go home, except Philip, who would not come among them.

"But before I go any further, I would take leave to mention a few remarkable passages of Providence which I took special notice of in my afflicted time." Mary devotes several pages to these "remarkable passages," some regarding the English army and what she perceived as lost opportunities for rescue. She also reflects on the ability of her captors to subsist on meager fare.

"Their chief and commonest food was ground-nuts; they ate also nuts and acorns, artichokes, lily-roots, ground-beans, and several other weeds and roots that I know not.

"They would pick up old bones and cut them in pieces at the joints, and, if they were full of worms and maggots, they would scald them over the fire to make the vermin come out, and then boil them and drink up the liquor, and then beat the great ends of them in a mortar and so eat them. They would eat horse's guts and ears and all sorts of wild birds, which they could catch--also bear, venison, beavers, tortoise, frogs, squirrels, dogs, skunks, rattlesnakes, yea, the very barks of trees, besides all sorts of creatures and provision which they plundered from the English.

"...But to return again to my going home...

"About the sun's going down, Mr. Hoar and myself, and the two Indians, came to Lancaster, and a solemn sight it was to me. There had I lived many comfortable years among my relations and neighbors, and now not one Christian to be seen nor one house left standing." They move on and spend the night at a farmhouse. The next day "before noon we came to Concord. Now was I full of joy and yet not without sorrow to see such a lovely sight, so many Christians together and some of them my neighbors.

"There I met with my brother [Josiah White] and my brother-in-law [Lieutenant Henry Kerley], who asked me if I knew where his wife was. Poor heart! He had helped to bury her and knew it not; she, being shot down by the house, was partly burnt, so that those who were at Boston at the desolation of the town, and came back afterward and buried the dead, did not know her. Yet I was not without sorrow to think how many were looking and longing, and my own children amongst the rest, to enjoy that deliverance that I had now received; and I did not know whether I should ever see them again.

"Being recruited with food and raiment, we went to Boston that day, where I met with my dear husband; but the thoughts of our dear children, one being dead, and the others we could not tell where, abated our comfort in each other. I was not before so much hemmed in with the merciless and cruel heathen, but now as much with pitiful, tender-hearted, and compassionate Christians. In that poor and distressed and beggarly condition I was received in, I was kindly entertained in several houses; so much love I received from several (some of whom I knew and others I knew not) that I am not capable to declare it...

"The twenty pounds, the price of my redemption, was raised by some Boston gentlemen and Mr. [Hezekiah] Usher [a Boston merchant], whose bounty and religious charity I would not forget to make mention of. Then Mr. Thomas Shepard of Charlestown received us into his house, where we continued eleven weeks--and a father and mother they were unto us. And many more tender-hearted friends we met with in that place. We were now in the midst of love, yet not without much and frequent heaviness of heart for our poor children and other relations who were still in affliction.

"The week following, after my coming in, the Governor and Council sent forth to the Indians again--and that not without success, for they brought in my sister and Goodwife Kettle. Their not knowing where our children were was a sore trial to us still, and yet we were not without secret hopes that we should see them again. That which was dead lay heavier upon my spirit than those which were alive amongst the heathen--thinking how it suffered with its wounds and I was no way able to relieve it, and how it was buried by the heathen in the wilderness, away from among all Christians.

"...Being unsettled in our minds, we thought we would ride toward the eastward to see if we could hear anything concerning our children. And as we were riding along...between Ipswich and Rowley, we met with Mr. William Hubbard, who told us our son, Joseph, was come to Major [Richard] Waldron's, and another with him, which was my sister's son [William Divoll]. I asked him how he knew it. He said the Major himself told him so. [See "Stratagem and Stealth" in Section Three for more about Major Waldron (Walderne).]

"So along we went till we came to Newbury; and, their minister being absent, they desired my husband to preach the Thanksgiving for them. But he was not willing to stay there that night, but would go over to Salisbury to hear farther and come again in the morning--which he did and preached there that day. At night, when he had done, one came and told him that his daughter was come in at Providence...

"Now we were between them: the one on the east and the other on the west. Our son being nearest, we went to him first, to Portsmouth, where we met with him and with the Major also, who told us he had done what he could, but could not redeem him under seven pounds, which the good people thereabouts were pleased to pay. The Lord reward the Major and all the rest, though unknown to me, for their labor of love. [The major eventually got his just deserts, but not in the way Mary hoped; see "Stratagem and Stealth."]

"My sister's son was redeemed for four pounds, which the Council gave order for the payment of. Having now received one of our children, we hastened toward the other; going back through Newbury, my husband preached there on the Sabboth day, for which they rewarded him manifold. On Monday we came to Charlestown, where we heard that the Governor of Rhode Island [William Coddington, the first governor of Rhode Island (1640-1647, re-elected 1674-1676). Born in England in 1601, he died in 1678.] had sent over for our daughter, to take care of her, being now within his jurisdiction--which should not pass without our acknowledgments. But she being nearer Rehoboth than Rhode Island, Mr. Newman went over and took care of her, and brought her to his own house."

The Reverend Noah Newman--not your typical minister--deserves further mention here because of his actions early in the war. Shortly after the outbreak of hostilities he organized a company of volunteers to pursue Philip and Weetamoo. Together with a band of fifty Mohegans under Oneco and volunteers from Providence, he attacked Weetamoo and her followers at Nipsachuck (Smithfield, Rhode Island). Although many enemy Indians were killed, Weetamoo escaped.

"The Indians were now gone that way [back to Plymouth Colony], that it was apprehended dangerous to go to her; but the carts which carried provisions to the English army, being guarded, brought her with them to Dorchester, where we received her safe...

"Her coming in was after this manner: she was traveling one day with the Indians, with her basket at her back. The company of Indians were got before her and gone out of sight, all except one squaw; she followed the squaw till night, and then both of them lay down, having nothing over them but the heavens, nor under them but the earth. Thus she traveled three days together, not knowing whither she was going, having nothing to eat or drink but water and green hirtleberries. At last they came to Providence, where she was kindly entertained by several of that town. The Indians often said that I should never have her under twenty pounds, but now the Lord hath brought her in upon free cost and given her to me the second time."

Mary devotes the next several pages to, and closes the book with, musings on religion. "I can remember the time when I used to sleep quietly, without workings in my thoughts, whole nights together; but now it is otherwise with me. When all are fast about me and no eye open but his who ever waketh, my thoughts are upon things past, upon the awful dispensations of the Lord toward us, upon his wonderful power and might in carrying us through so many difficulties, in returning us in safety and suffering none to hurt us..."

Harpies, Housewives,
and Heroines

Slipping away from the rest of the party with her five-year-old child, she found that she could indeed make the damaged craft seaworthy. And thus, by a thread, she effected their escape.--Russell Bourne, The Red King's Rebellion

The Heroic Girl at the Door

The following incident occurred on October 1, 1675. The account is taken from *The Young People's History of Maine* by Geo. J. Varney, published in 1874.

"The next attack was at Newichawannock [South Berwick], on the house of John Tozer, who had gone with Captain [John] Wincoll, leaving his family unprotected. His was one of the outermost houses of the settlement; and in it were gathered at that moment fifteen women and children. A young lady of eighteen was the first to discover the Indians. She had only time to warn the family, when the savages reached the house. Fearful that the weak door fastenings would give way, she staid and held them until the hatchets of the savages had broken through.

"They dashed in the door; but the family had escaped from the other side of the house, and were running toward the garrison. A part of the Indians pursued them, catching two children who were hindmost. One of these, only three years old, they killed on the spot; and the other they kept in captivity six months. But the heroic girl at the door--the savages were so angry at finding the house empty, they beat her to death, as they thought. After they had gone she revived, and lived to recover from her wounds. I wish I knew her name, for no personage in this history would more brightly ornament its pages."

Why it is that we know the age of the "young lady"--eighteen--but not her name, remains a mystery. As Bodge says in *Soldiers in King Philip's War*, "…it is to be regretted that Mr. [William] Hubbard, who relates this, did not record the name of the heroine, as he doubtless could have easily done."

The "savages" were Abenakis led by Hope Hood, sachem of the Norridgewock tribe of the Kennebecks. Hope Hood was noted for his cruelty toward prisoners. At one point he served as a slave in Boston. Throughout King Philip's War he continued to lead attacks against the English. In King William's War he sided with the French; he was killed in Canada in 1690, by Indians who mistook him for an Iroquois.

Stratagem and Stealth

Although women in the seventeenth century were neither warriors nor soldiers (not in New England, anyhow), they sometimes played important roles in helping to defeat the enemy. They prepared bandages, nursed the wounded, passed powder and ammunition, and even loaded muskets during attacks; on occasion English women may even have fired weapons from within besieged garrisons, if there were not enough men present to hold off the enemy.

Indian women, having fewer constraints imposed upon them by society than their English counterparts, were able to take on even more important assignments. Whereas it would be unheard of for English women, singly or in groups, to stroll into an Indian village unaccompanied by English men, Indian women frequently entered English towns by themselves or with only female companions, seeking work, or to trade, or simply a place to spend the night.

On rare occasions they might have a more sinister purpose for visiting a settlement, such as to spy on the unsuspecting English and report back to their leaders any strengths or weakness they observed. Or they might have an even more nefarious intent, as evinced by the following, from *The Young People's History of Maine* by Geo. J. Varney, published in 1874.

"Two days after this attack [upon the house of Anthony Brackett, by a group of Abenakis lead by Simon the Yankee-killer], a party of natives came at nightfall to the house of Richard Hammond at Stinson's Point in Woolwich, who gave the squaws permission to lodge on the kitchen floor. A girl of the family became so alarmed by certain tokens of malice and treachery among the squaws that she ran out of the house; but some of them brought her back and tried to allay her fears.

"A little after, she escaped again from the dwelling and hid in the cornfield. By and by she heard a great tumult in the house--heavy blows, shrieks, and the yells of warriors, whom the squaws had let in. At this the girl left her hiding place and fled to the nearest settlement on the mainland, twelve long miles away."

Having squaws approach a dwelling or fortress and ask to spend the night, thereby gaining entry, (after all, they were only women, what harm could they do?) for the purpose of unlatching the doors in the wee hours to let in a band of warriors, was a trick the Indians used time and again.

The English, apparently, were slow to catch on.

One notorious instance of this ploy occurred in 1689; I include an account of it here because although it took place during a later Indian war, it was a direct result of events in King Philip's War, and in a sense was a continuation of that conflict.

Major Richard Walderne, the richest and most powerful man in Maine and New Hampshire, through his harsh dealings with the Indians and his treacheries upon them (especially a number of betrayals of their trust during King Philip's War) had incurred their undying hatred. The following is taken from *Soldiers in King Philip's War*, by George Madison Bodge, Third Edition, published in Boston in 1906.

"In June, 1689, the people began to be aware of large numbers of strange Indians among those who came in to trade, and many did not seem to come for that purpose, but were observed carefully scrutinizing the defenses and approaches. The people became alarmed, and one after another many came and urged Major Walderne to take some precautions of defense. He, however, would not hearken, laughed at their fears, and told them to 'go and plant their pumpkins,' and he would tell them when the Indians should attack them.

"There were many old friends of the Major and of the English of Dover among the neighboring Indians, and some of these tried to warn them of the danger. A squaw came through the town, and here and there significantly recited the words which have been handed down in the rhyme,

'O Major Waldron, you great sagamore,
What will you do, Indians at your door.'

"Captain Thomas Henchman of Chelmsford also was apprised of the plot against Dover, and sent a letter of warning to the Council of Boston. [The Council sent urgent messengers to Dover, but they, unfortunately for the Major, arrived a day too late.]

"On the evening of the 27th two squaws applied at each of the garrison houses for permission to sleep inside, as was often done, and two were admitted into each of the garrisons, Walderne's, Heard's, and Otis's, and were shown how to unfasten the gates if they wished to go away during the night. There was a report of a great number of Indians coming to trade next day, and the sachem Wesandowit, who had taken supper at the Major's, asked him pointedly, 'Brother Waldron, what would you do if the strange Indians should come?'

"'I could assemble a hundred men by lifting up my finger,' replied the Major, in careless indifference. And thus all retired to rest; no watch was placed and no precautions taken.

"After midnight the gates were opened by the squaws. The Indians waiting outside rushed in and took possession without any alarm and rushed into the Major's room."

Needless to say, the Indians took their revenge upon the eighty-year-old Walderne, killing him in a rather gruesome fashion.

❧

The important roles sometimes played by Indian women in helping to take fortified positions did not end with the wars in New England. Nearly a hundred years later, during Pontiac's

Rebellion, hostile Indians were able to capture a fort by the following stratagem.

A group of Indians approached the fortress, pretending to be friendly and wishing to trade. The wary soldiers inside granted them permission to enter, but only on the condition that the warriors lay down their weapons beforehand. This the men did; the gates were opened and the unarmed men went inside, followed by the women in their group.

The women were draped in blankets. Concealed under the blankets they carried hatchets and other weapons. At a prearranged signal the women handed the weapons to the men, who then overpowered the soldiers and took the fort.

Escape by Needle and Thread

No doubt Ann Brackett, like most English women in New England in the seventeenth century, especially those living on the frontier, made and mended much of the clothing worn by herself and her family. She may even had made some of the cloth from which the clothing was fashioned. In any event she was, as we shall see, skilled with needle and thread, although the use to which she put both was somewhat unconventional.

The following is taken from *The Story of Old Falmouth* by James Otis, published in 1901. (The Falmouth of the title is present-day Portland, Maine.)

"On the 9th of August, 1676, a well-known Indian named Simon [who as we learned in a previous chapter had achieved the epithet "the Yankee-killer"], who had been imprisoned at Dover [New Hampshire] awaiting his trial on the charge of murder, appeared at the farm-house of Anthony Brackett [located on Portland's Back Cove], and was accused by him of having stolen a cow a few days previous. Simon denied the charge, but promised to bring the culprits to Mr. Brackett's home on the third day. Agreeably to the promise he came, accompanied by five other Indians, and was admitted to the house by Mr. Brackett himself, who had no suspicion that mischief was intended. Then began the work of murder…

"Regarding this attack, there is in the collection of the Massachusetts Historical Society a letter from Thaddeus Clark, written to his mother in Boston. In this letter the unfortunate man says:

"'On Friday morning your own son with your sons-in-law, Anthony and Thomas Brackett, and their whole families were killed or taken captives by the Indians. It is certain that Thomas was slain, and his wife and children carried away, but of Anthony and his family we have no tidings, therefore think they may have been captured the night before, for, as you know, they live at a long distance from any neighbor.'

[Anthony, his wife Ann, with at least one of their children, and a black servant had indeed been captured by Simon and the others. Although the remainder of Thaddeus's letter to his mother does not directly bear on their plight, it is of sufficient interest to be included in this chapter.]

"'Mr. Corbin and all his family; Mr. Lewis and his wife; James Ross and family; Mr. Durham, John Murphy, Daniel Wakely, Benjamin Hadwell and his family were all killed before the sun was an hour high in the morning. Mr. Wallis's house was the only one burned. There are of men slain, eleven; of women and children killed and taken, twenty-three. We that are alive are forced upon Mr. Andrews on his island to secure our own and the lives of our families.

"'We have but little provisions, and are so few in number that we are not able to bury the dead until more strength comes to us. We entreat the Governor that forthwith aid may be sent to us, either to fight the enemy out of our borders that our English corn may be planted whereby we may live comfortably, or remove us out of danger that we may provide for ourselves elsewhere. Desiring your prayers to God for His preservation of us in these times of danger, I rest Your dutiful son, Thaddeus Clark.'"

Geo. J. Varney, in *The Young People's History of Maine*, tells the rest of the story.

"One day Francis Card, who had been captured in Woolwich, was sent with another prisoner to find a horse and drive him to be killed; but they found a canoe instead of a horse, and quickly made their escape. Simon, the Yankee-killer, had gone to other scenes of violence [Arrowsic, on the Kennebec], leaving the family of Anthony Brackett [in a camp on the north side of Casco Bay] to follow, not supposing that they could by any means escape; but they found on the shore a leaky birchen canoe; and Mrs. Brackett [using a needle and thread found in the camp] repaired it so well that they all embarked, and reached Scarborough in safety."

William Hubbard, a clergyman living in Massachusetts, wrote a history of the war titled *A Narrative of the Troubles with the Indians in New-England*, published in Boston in 1677 and, slightly revised, in London that same year. He included the story of Ann Brackett, and made it clear that it was she, through her courage and resourcefulness, as well as her skill with needle and thread, rather than her husband or their male servant, who deserved the credit for their escape to freedom.

Signal by Pounding

The loneliness of women living on the frontier during wartime, with men off working in the fields, or worse, hundreds of miles away fighting the enemy, can only be imagined. Women sometimes came up with ingenious ways for relieving that loneliness. The following is taken from *Home Life in Colonial Days* by Alice Morse Earle.

"The Indian method of preparing maize or corn was to steep or parboil it in hot water for twelve hours, then to pound the grain in a mortar or a hollowed stone in the field, till it was a coarse meal. It was then sifted in a rather closely woven basket, and the large grains which did not pass through the sieve were again pounded and sifted.

"Samp [hominy] was often pounded in olden times in a primitive and picturesque Indian mortar made of a hollowed block of wood or a stump of a large tree, which had been cut off about three feet from the ground. The pestle was a heavy block of wood shaped like the inside of the mortar, and fitted with a handle attached to one side. This block was fastened to the top of a young and slender tree, a growing sapling, which was bent over and thus gave a sort of spring which pulled the pestle up after being pounded down on the corn. This was called a sweep and mortar mill.

"They could be heard at a long distance. Two New Hampshire pioneers made clearings about a quarter of a mile apart and built houses. There was an impenetrable gully and thick woods between the cabins; and the blazed path was a long distance around, so the wives of the settlers seldom saw each other or any other woman. It was a source of great comfort and companionship to them both that they could signal to each other every day by pounding on their mortars. And they had an ingenious system of communication which one spring morning summoned one to the home of the other, where she arrived in time to be the first to welcome fine twin babies."

Hurrah for Hannah!

The English settlement of Northampton, in the Connecticut River Valley, was attacked by Indians several times, at least twice in October, 1675, and again in March, 1676. In a later chapter I address the issue of stress experienced by women attempting to go about their daily routines, which were sufficiently burdensome even in times of peace. With a full-scale war of annihilation being waged around them, one might think that fashion, in the matter of attire, might be least from most people's thoughts.

Not so.

The following is taken from *Home Life in Colonial Days* by Alice Morse Earle.

"In England extravagance in dress in court circles, and grotesqueness in dress among all educated folk, had become abhorrent to that class of persons who were called Puritans; and as an expression of their dislike they wore plainer garments, and cut off their flowing locks, and soon were called Roundheads.

"The Massachusetts settlers who were Puritans determined to discourage extravagance in dress in the New World, and attempted to control the fashions. The Massachusetts magistrates were reminded of their duties in this direction by sanctimonious spurring from gentlemen and ministers in England. One such meddler wrote to Governor Winthrop in 1636: 'Many in your plantation discover too much pride.'

"In 1634 the Massachusetts General Court passed restricting sumptuary laws. These laws forbade the purchase of woolen, silk, or linen garments, with silver, gold, silk, or thread lace on them. Two years later a narrow binding of lace was permitted on linen garments. The colonists were ordered not to make or buy any slashed clothes, except those with one slash in each sleeve and another slash in the back. 'Cut works, embroidered or needle or cap bands & rails,' and gold or silver girdles, hatbands, belts, ruffs, and beaver hats were forbidden. Liberty was thriftily given, however, to the colonists to wear out any garments they chanced to have unless in the form of inordinately slashed apparel, immoderately great sleeves and rails, and long wings, which could not possibly be endured.

"In Northampton, in the year 1676, a wholesale attempt was made by the magistrates to abolish 'wicked apparel.' Thirty-eight women of the Connecticut valley were 'presented' at one time for various degrees of finery, and as of too small estate [i.e., not wealthy enough] to wear silk. A young girl named Hannah Lyman was presented for 'wearing silk in a flaunting manner, in an offensive way and garb not only before but when she stood presented.' The calm flaunting of her silk in the very eyes of the Court by sixteen-year-old Hannah was premonitory of the waning power of the magistrates, for similar prosecutions at a later date were quashed."

The Gentler Sex?

In the summer of 1676, with the death of Philip at Mount Hope on August 12, and the capture of his field commander Anawan in Rehoboth on August 28, the war in southern New England was essentially over, save for the rounding up (i.e., the massacre, capture, execution, and sale into slavery) of hundreds of starving and demoralized Indians.

Gradually, English settlers returned to their homes, or what was left of them. In the meantime the war continued in the north, in Maine, New Hampshire, and southern Vermont.

Mugg Hegone, sachem of the Androscoggins, and one of the more capable of the northern Indian leaders, desired to return the war to the south; he conceived no less an objective than the burning of Boston. "We must go to the fishing islands and take all the white man's vessels," he advised. With this fleet the Abenakis would sail into Boston Harbor and drive the English out. It was a brilliant idea--except that the Indians had little or no experience in sailing ships. Geo. J. Varney, in *The Young People's History of Maine*, relates what happened.

"When the time of year came for Bay fishing, the savages proceeded to execute this plan. In the daytime they prowled along the shores, spying out their prey; and in the darkness of night they slid out noiselessly in their light canoes, boarding the motionless vessels, and killing or capturing their sleeping crews. In the month of July they secured about twenty vessels, each of them having a crew of from three to six men. When these captures became known, a large ship was sent after them. She was supplied with plenty of cannon and small arms, and manned by forty seamen and sailors.

"It was expected that this vessel would somewhere encounter the Indian fleet, which she would capture or sink, and at the same time destroy a multitude of savages. She came upon the vessels--one here, another there--some aground, and others beating against the rocks. But not an Indian in any of them. The vessels were so large they could not be navigated by paddles; and the sails flew and flapped about, while the vessels went in any direction but that which their dusky sailors desired; consequently they soon abandoned the prizes in fright and disgust."

One evening that same month (July, 1677) a boat appeared in Marblehead Harbor. In it were a group of fisherman from the area, whose ship was among those seized by the Indians. The men had managed to escape, and were returning home, bringing with them two Abenaki captives, whom they intended to sell as slaves to help pay for their stolen vessel.

When the men reached shore they were met by an angry crowd, bent on revenge against the two hapless Indians [as if slavery was not punishment enough!]. One of the fishermen, Robert Roules, later recounted what happened

"The whole town flocked about them, beginning at first to insult them, and soon after, the women surrounded them… and laid violent hands upon the captives, some stoning us in the meantime, because we would protect them, others seizing them by the hair…Then with stones, billets of wood, and what else they might, they made an end of these Indians…We found them with their heads off and gone, and their flesh in a manner pulled from their bones. And such was the tumulation these women made, that for my life I could not tell who these women were, or the names of any of them."

And Varney referred to the Indians as "savages!" Heaven defend us from the women of Marblehead. The fisherman was wise to profess not to recognize or know the names of any of them.

The Milk of Human Kindness

A much pleasanter story than that involving the women of Marblehead--though not without poignancy--concerns an interchange that took place between an English woman, Dinah Fenner, and a Narragansett squaw whose name has not come down to us.

In the collection of the Rhode Island Historical Society in Providence there is preserved a basket, humble in origin but of great historical, as well as symbolic, significance, as we shall see.

At some point toward the end of the war a Narragansett squaw, hungry, perhaps starving, approached the Fenner Garrison in Cranston and asked for food. Although the folks within the garrison had little enough provisions for themselves, Dinah Fenner offered the squaw some milk. The unfortunate woman had nothing with which to repay this act of kindness except a dilapidated basket. Nothing daunted, she went down to the river, and with strips of bark obtained from a basswood tree repaired the basket, which she then gave to Dinah in gratitude.

There is a variation of the story, imaginative but perhaps possessing a modicum of truth, which maintains that the reason why the squaw repaired the basket was because it was the only container she had, and in its damaged condition would not hold liquid, the squaw desirous of carrying the milk outside with her, perhaps to feed a child. In any event, in the end she gave the basket to Dinah, who must have valued it greatly, for it to have been preserved in the family for so many years.

Penelope Winslow

In striking contrast to the hardships and dangers endured by women living on the frontier, Penelope Pelham Winslow lived a life of relative ease and security. The daughter of Jemima Waldegrave and Herbert Pelham, she was born in England in 1633, a member of the gentry. Her father practiced law at Gray's Inn in London; her mother was an heiress. Penelope's maternal grandparents, Margaret and Thomas Waldegrave, lived in a many-roomed mansion with forty-four fireplaces; Queen Elizabeth I had visited there at least twice.

Herberet Pelham, a staunch Puritan, along with his father-in-law joined the Massachusetts Bay Company in 1629, but did not move to Massachusetts until 1638, when Penelope was five. Her mother became ill and died, apparently before reaching New England. In Cambridge her father bought a house near Harvard, where, in 1643, he became the college's first treasurer. In 1646, when Penelope was thirteen, she returned with her father to England, where she remained an unknown number of years. Her father never returned to New England; he became a justice of the peace and a member of Parliament, and died in 1674 at the age of seventy-four.

Penelope married Josiah Winslow, son of the Pilgrim Edward Winslow. (Edward was the third governor of Plymouth Colony and a friend of Massasoit, Philip's father.) Whether she married Josiah in England or in New England is not known, nor in what year. In 1658 the couple were living at Careswell, the extensive Winslow estate in Marshfield, Plymouth Colony, where Penlope gave birth to their first child. There, as in England, she did not lack physical comforts. There were servants to do the work, ample furnishings to use and enjoy, and luxurious personal possessions, such as bottles with pewter tops and combs made from ivory. (Many of these items are on display at the Plymouth Hall Museum in Plymouth.)

Like Mary Rowlandson's, albeit under far different circumstances, Penelope Winslow's path was destined to cross that of Weetamoo. Although English gentlewoman and squaw sachem lived worlds apart, if not literally then figuratively and culturally, fate--for one of them, *cruel* fate--would bring them, however briefly, together.

Josiah Winslow was born in Plymouth Colony in 1629, the eldest son of Edward Winslow (governor in 1633, again in 1636, and once more in 1644) and his second wife, Susanna (Fuller) White, mother by her first marriage of Peregrine White, the first English child born in Plymouth Colony. Josiah attended Harvard but did not graduate, leaving instead in 1650 to join his father in England. In 1659, having in the interim returned to New England, he became commander-in-chief of Plymouth Colony's military, the post previously held by Myles Standish.

In 1662 an event occurred that greatly increased the Wampanoags' growing resentment of the English, and was, in all probability, a contributing factor to the outbreak of war thirteen years later. Since it was this occurrence that led to the probable meeting of Penlope and Weetamoo, a full account of it is included here.

The following is taken, with some minor changes, from the writings of Increase Mather, father of Cotton Mather, as quoted in Samuel D. Drake's *Biography and History of the Indians of North America*, published in Boston in 1841. [In reading this account we must keep in mind that Mather was, to put it mildly, biased against the Indians, as well as indifferent to the idea of giving women their proper due in history.]

"In A. D. 1662, Plymouth Colony was in some danger of being involved in trouble by the Wampanoag Indians. After Massasoit was dead [around 1661], his two sons, called

Wamsutta and Metacomet, came to the court at Plymouth, pretending high respect for the English, and, therefore, desired English names might be imposed on them, whereupon the court there named Wamsutta, the elder brother, Alexander, and Metacomet, the younger brother, Philip.

"This Alexander, Philip's immediate predecessor, was not so faithful and friendly to the English as his father had been. For some of Boston, having been occasionally at Narragansett, wrote to Mr. Prince [Thomas Prence], who was then governor of Plymouth Colony, that Alexander was contriving mischief against the English, and that he had solicited the Narragansetts to engage with him in his designed rebellion. Hereupon, Captain Willet [Thomas Willet, who became the first English mayor of New York City], who lived near Mount Hope, the place where Alexander resided, was appointed to speak with him, and to desire him to attend the next court in Plymouth, for their satisfaction, and his own vindication.

"He seemed to take the message in good part, professing that the Narragansetts, who, he said, were his enemies, had put an abuse upon him, and he readily promised to attend the next court. But when the day for his appearance was come, instead of that, he at that very time went over to the Narragansetts, his pretended enemies, which, compared with other circumstances, caused the gentlemen at Plymouth to suspect there was more of truth in the information given, than at first they were aware of. Wherefore the governor and magistrates there ordered Major Winslow to take a party of men, and fetch down Alexander. The major [accompanied by William Bradford, Jr.] took but ten armed men with him from Marshfield, intending to have taken more at the towns that lay nearer Mount Hope. But when they were about midway between Plymouth and Bridgewater [at Monponset Pond in Halifax], observing a hunting house, they rode up to it, and there found Alexander and many of his men well armed, but their guns standing together without the house.

"Winslow, with his small party, possessed themselves of the Indians' arms, and beset the house; then he went in amongst them, acquainting the sachem with the reason of his coming; desiring Alexander with his interpreter to walk out with him, who did so a little distance from the house, and then understood what commission the major had received concerning him. The proud sachem fell into a raging passion at this surprise, saying the governor had no reason to credit rumors, or to send for him in such a way, nor would he go to Plymouth, but when he saw cause.

"The major told him that his order was to bring him to Plymouth, and that, by the help of God, he would do it, or else he would die on the place; also declaring to him that if he would submit, he might expect respective usage, but if he once more denied to go, he should never stir from the ground whereupon he stood; and with a pistol at the sachem's breast, required that his next words should be a positive and clear answer to what he demanded.

"Alexander yielded to go, only requesting that he might go like a sachem, with his men attending him, which, although there was some hazard in it, they being many, and the English but a few, was granted to him. The weather being hot, the major offered him a horse to ride upon, but his squaw [Weetamoo] and divers Indian women being in company, he refused, saying he could go on foot, as well as they, which was done. And resting several times by the way, Alexander and his Indians were refreshed by the English. No other discourse happening while they were upon their march, but what was pleasant and amicable.

"The major sent a man before, to entreat that as many of the magistrates of that colony as could would meet at Duxbury. Wherefore having there had some treaty with Alexander, not willing to commit him to prison, they entreated Major Winslow to receive him to his house, until the governor, who then lived at Eastham, could come up.

"Accordingly, Alexander and his train were courteously entertained by the major [and, we may assume, by his wife Penelope; we can only speculate on how she received Weetamoo, and whether the two women enjoyed any interaction]. And albeit, not so much as an angry word passed between them whilst at Marshfield; yet proud Alexander, vexing and fuming in his spirit, that such a check was given him, he suddenly fell sick of a fever. He was then nursed as a choice friend. Mr. [Matthew] Fuller, the physician, coming providently thither at that time, the sachem and his men earnestly desired that he would administer to him; he therefore gave him a portion of working physic, which the Indians thought did him good.

"But his distemper afterwards prevailing, they entreated to dismiss him, in order to return home, which upon encouragement of appearance at the next court was granted him. Soon after his being returned home he died."

The death of Alexander.

As mentioned in a previous chapter, Weetamoo and Philip always believed that the English deliberately poisoned Alexander.

Accounts vary, but there may have been as many as eighty men and women (and children?) in Alexander's party. As "guests" at Careswell, would Alexander and Weetamoo have been invited into the house? For meals? To spend the night? Alexander was after all the son of Massasoit, the man who in 1621 saved the Pilgrims from almost certain death from starvation, the man whom Josiah's father, Edward, considered a close friend.

Most likely they would have camped outside, under some sort of guard. Weetamoo and Penelope would have at least caught a glimpse of one another; any other discourse that might have occurred between them is purely speculative. Was Penelope gracious toward her Indian counterpart? Haughty? Indifferent? Was Weetamoo sullen? outraged? by the unjust treatment her husband, Great Sachem of all the Wampanoags, had received at the hands of the son of his father's former friend? We'll never know. Historians of the day--Increase Mather, William Hubbard, and a handful of others--who took the time to write about incidents in the war, and those leading up to it, sadly neglected to mention, except in passing, the roles played by women.

When, in 1675, the long-anticipated war finally broke out, it was Philip, Alexander's younger brother, who led the uprising against the English. In the early phases of the war Josiah Winslow was commander-in-chief of the United Colonies' forces. (The United Colonies--Plymouth, Massachusetts Bay, and Connecticut--had an agreement, that in whichever colony their forces were deployed, the leader of that colony's army would be commander-in-chief of all.) For reasons of health, Josiah relinquished command in 1676. In the meantime, in 1673, he had become governor of Plymouth Colony, the first native-born governor in America. It was a position he held until1680, when he died at the age of fifty-two.

In July, 1675, shortly after hostilities broke out, Careswell being considered unsafe, Penelope took her two children, Elizabeth aged thirteen and Isaac aged five, to Salem, where she stayed with her sister-in-law, Elizabeth Corwin. Not all women in New England were so fortunate as to be able to relocate with their children to a place of safety. Most women, in fact, were forbidden to do so. There were practical as well as financial obstacles, of course. In the seventeenth century travel for women--assuming there was any household willing, and able, to accept them--was extremely difficult, not to mention dangerous, even in normal times. Moreover, to prevent settlements from becoming partially or wholly deserted, and thereby easy targets for the enemy, the colonies, at various times, passed laws prohibiting families from leaving their homes and moving elsewhere, with severe penalties if they did so.

Most women, therefore, especially those living in frontier settlements, but even those living in more established communities, remained vulnerable, all the more so in view of the fact that many of the able-bodied men who under ordinary circumstances might be called upon to defend them, were absent, away fighting, or worse, killed or severely wounded.

In December, 1675, with repeated attacks against the English occurring in exposed areas of Plymouth Colony (Middleborough and Old Dartmouth, the latter including what are now New Bedford and Fairhaven, having been destroyed as early as July), and the war having spread into Massachusetts (the Nipmucks, Pocumtucks, Agawams and other tribes having joined the Wampanoags, with the severest fighting taking place in the Connecticut River Valley), and northern New England (the Abenakis attacking settlements as early as September 5th), the United Colonies, distrustful of the Narragansetts, the most powerful Indian tribe in New England, invaded their territory in Rhode Island--first notifying the government of Rhode Island of their intention, but not asking permission.

On December 19th, the English, with an army consisting of at least a thousand English and one hundred and fifty

Mohegans and Pequots, with Josiah Winslow in command, attacked the fort in Kingston where the Narragansetts, along with several hundred Wampanoag women and children to whom they had given refuge, had set up camp for the winter. There is no need to repeat the details of the fight, except to mention, once again, that the English, besides killing hundreds of Narragansett warriors, massacred many more hundreds of women and children, while themselves suffering considerable losses.

After the fight Winslow's army made its weary way back to its base at Smith's Castle in Wickford (mentioned elsewhere, in the chapter titled "Quaiapen"and in the Appendix subtitled "The Queen's Fort"). The Connecticut troops, in dissension with the others, soon returned home. Short of food, and suffering from the harsh winter, Winslow at the end of January took his remaining forces in pursuit of the enemy, camping outside of Providence before moving northward into Nipmuck country. Meanwhile many of his men deserted. Those who remained suffered greatly from hunger and exposure. (At one point the English killed and ate their horses.) Although they engaged the enemy on several occasions, no decisive battle took place. Finally, on February 5th Winslow brought his Plymouth and Massachusetts forces into Boston. There they disbanded.

Evidently Josiah never fully recovered from the adverse effects of his ordeal. As already stated, he left Penelope a widow in 1680. She was forty-seven years old. Elizabeth, their daughter, was sixteen, and Isaac eleven. Penelope, wealthy, never remarried. She lived at Careswell with her children. In 1684 Elizabeth married. Isaac went to Harvard, and afterwards became a prominent judge and a colonel in the militia.

In 1699 he built a fine new mansion in Marshfield, naming it, too, Careswell. (This "new" Careswell is extant, and open to the public. Many events of historical interest are held there; a few years ago I gave a talk on King Philip's War to a packed audience.) Here Penelope spent the remainder of her days. In 1700 Isaac married Sarah Wensley; in 1701 their son,

Penelope's first grandchild, was born: named Josiah, after his paternal grandfather.

Penelope died two years later, in 1703, at the age of seventy.

As a sidebar to the story of Penelope Winslow, let us consider the mystery surrounding the fate of King Philip's wampum belts.

Philip was hunted down by Benjamin Church and shot dead by one of Church's Indian soldiers at Mount Hope on August 12, 1676. On August 28, Church surprised and captured Philip's field commander Anawan at his campsite in Rehoboth. The following excerpt, from Benjamin Church's *Entertaining Passages Relating to King Philip's War*, relates how, during the night, Anawan got up from his position next to Church, only to return a few minutes later.

"The moon now shining bright, he [Church] saw him at a distance coming with something in his hands, and coming up to Captain Church, he fell upon his knees before him and offered him what he'd brought, and speaking in plain English, said, 'Great Captain, you have killed Philip, and conquered his country, for I believe, that I and my company are the last that war against the English, so suppose the war is ended by your means, and therefore these things belong unto you.'

"Then opening his pack, he pulled out Philip's belt curiously wrought with wampum, in various figures and flowers, and pictures of many birds and beasts. This when hung upon Captain Church's shoulders reached his ankles. And another belt of wampum he presented him with, wrought after the former manner, which Philip was wont to put upon his head; it had two flags on the back part which hung down on his back: and another small belt with a star upon the end of it, which he used to hang on his breast; and they were all edged with red hair, which Anawan said they got in the Mohawk country."

Benjamin Church dutifully presented the belts to Josiah Winslow.

What happened then?

The following, with some changes, is taken from my *Ghosts from King Philip's War*, published in 2006.

"A mystery surrounds the ultimate fate and present whereabouts (if they still exist) of Philip's wampum belts. These elaborately beaded belts, described in the passage above, were customarily worn ceremonially by Philip as a symbol of his authority. They were reputed to have been of great beauty and workmanship, and of great worth.

"With the cessation of hostilities, Josiah Winslow cast his eyes on the lands around Mount Hope. At the same time, in 1677, Plymouth Colony found itself in somewhat of an awkward situation, in that it lacked a royal charter defining its exact boundaries. Even before the war, disputes among the colonies had frequently arisen as to precisely where one colony ended and another began. How best to secure those boundaries while making a claim against Philip's former domain?

"To compound the issue, the other colonies--especially Rhode Island--were blaming Plymouth for having provoked the war in the first place.

"Winslow hit upon the idea of writing to the king [Charles II] of England. In his letter he would explain the causes of the war, make it clear to the crown that Plymouth had not been the aggressor, and incidentally assert Plymouth's right to the conquered territory. With the letter he would include a gift to the king: the three wampum belts that had been worn by Philip as a symbol of his authority.

"It was a significant gift. Even if the wampum belts had not once belonged to the vanquished Philip, they would still have been extremely valuable for their intrinsic worth.

"Wampum consisted of beads made from the shells of quahogs (hardshelled clams), whelks, and periwinkles. The beads were strung together, often in elaborate patterns. Philip's were especially ornate, with depictions of flowers, birds, and animals, as well as other decorative motifs.

"Governor Winslow--unwisely it turned out--asked his brother-in-law, Major Waldegrave Pelham, to deliver the letter along with the wampum belts to the king. Neither belts nor letter have been seen since.

[Penelope Pelham was the fifth of six siblings. Her parents' first child, Waldegrave, was born in 1627. The details of his life are sketchy. When Penelope, her father, and her sisters sailed for New England in 1638, Waldegrave remained behind. He studied law at London's Inner Temple, and married in 1649.]

"In 1679 the unsuspecting Winslow received a rather testy letter from the king asking why he had neglected so long to send a report of the war to England. It was only then that the governor realized that his brother-in-law had failed to deliver the letter and belts, as promised, to the king. Fortunately the king accepted Winslow's explanation of the matter, and graciously (or perhaps sardonically) thanked him for the gifts which he had never received. Plymouth Colony obtained the Mount Hope peninsula, which it promptly sold to four Massachusetts proprietors, and the town of Bristol was established.

"Winslow never actually accused his brother-in-law of theft (so as to keep peace in the family?), but the assumption is that Waldegrave Pelham kept the wampum belts for himself. What became of the original letter is anyone's guess. (A copy eventually made its way to the king.) As for the belts--what ultimately became of them? Did Waldegrave take them apart and use the strings of wampum (which even individually were of great value) for his own purposes? Or did he hide them somewhere, with the intention of selling them at a later date?

"One theory holds that he buried them near his estate in Essex, England. Another maintains that the British crown (knowingly or unknowingly) is in possession of them, possibly at the Tower of London. Still another holds faith that they are among the vast holdings of the British Museum.

"We'll probably never know what became of Philip's wampum belts, but the hope, slender though it be, remains that someday, somehow, they will be found in some hidden recess, or tucked away in some secret corner, and placed in a museum for all to appreciate and enjoy."

Since writing the above, I've had additional thoughts about the matter. In 1677 Josiah Winslow knew that his health was failing. As a staunch Puritan, he had no love for the monarchy. Charles II was the son of Charles I, whom the victorious Parliamentary faction, backed by the Puritans, had beheaded at the end of England's Civil War. England was a long sea voyage away from Plymouth Colony. Waldegrave Pelham was the brother of his beloved wife, Penelope.

It's idle to speculate--but one wonders...

Wootonekanuske

Wootonekanuske, Philip's wife, was the daughter of Corbitant and the younger sister of Weetamoo. Little has come down to us regarding her, except for the details of her capture by the English and her probable ultimate fate. Daniel Strock, Jr., in *Pictorial History of King Philip's War*, tells us the story:

"Early on the morning of the 31st [of July, 1676, Captain Benjamin] Church, with his own forces, and those of Bridgewater, marched to the Taunton River. On reaching the scene of the previous day's battle [in which Philip's uncle, Unkompoin, and his sister, believed to be Amie, were captured], he perceived an Indian seated on the stump of a tree which lay across the stream. Raising his gun, he took deliberate aim; but, at the moment that his finger touched the trigger, one of his Indians exclaimed that it was a friend. Church immediately lowered his gun, and the Indian, hearing the noise, turned his head. It was Philip. Church immediately raised his gun and fired. But it was too late. Philip threw himself off the log, and down the bank escaped.

"Church immediately crossed the log, and began a rapid pursuit. He was unable to overtake Philip or the Narragansetts, who scattered in every direction; but he picked up a number of women and children, among whom were the sachem's wife and his son, a lad nine years old.

"Let it not be supposed that because Philip's wife was taken he had deserted her. He was surprised when alone--mourning over the calamities of his tribe, unknowing where to go or what to do. At the report of Church's musket his people had scattered, and the chief, hurrying in their track, had no opportunity to secure either wife or child.

"The manner in which the reverend authors of that day exult over the capture of these helpless dependents of a heart-broken enemy, is characteristic of the spirit with which the colonists prosecuted this war.

"'Philip (says [Increase] Mather) hardly escaped with his life. He had fled; also his squaw and his son were taken captive, and are now prisoners at Plymouth. Thus hath God brought that grand enemy into great misery, before he quite destroy him. It must needs be bitter as death to him, to lose his wife and only son (for the Indians are marvelous fond and affectionate towards their children), besides other relations, and almost all his subjects, and country also.'

"And what were the feelings of the fugitive chief? 'My heart breaks,' were the mournful words that burst from his lips. It had been breaking since the treachery of Awashonks.

"The treatment which these two captives received forms a still sadder story. They were sent by Church to Bridgewater, and thence remanded to Plymouth. The Council, overjoyed at the opportunity of making examples of individuals so conspicuous, took their case into special consideration.

"When the mother and her child were arraigned the war was over. Philip was dead; the power of the New England tribes was gone forever. Surely the victors could spare the helpless, those who had taken no part in the war except to suffer by it. Let us observe what they did.

"Some clamored for blood. Hanging, shooting, beheading, were proposed. Court and people were in an uproar. They who suffered with Philip were pronounced guilty as those who fought for him. Fidelity in a woman, and innocence in a child, were, in the eyes of a Plymouth assembly, deemed crimes worthy of death.

"A few proposed milder measures. It could not be maintained, they argued, that he who accompanies a murderer through force or necessity, was equally guilty with one who voluntarily accompanies him. If the mother and her boy had not engaged in hostilities (of which proof appeared wanting), they could scarcely be considered as capital offenders. During the war some captive Indians, who were in the same situation, had been induced to join the army against their countrymen, and proved efficient soldiers. Though this mode of retaliation could not be resorted to in the present case, both because the war being over there was no further need of Indian help, and the age and sex of the prisoners forbade it, yet it afforded a precedent that every grade of crime should not be punished alike.

"What then was to be done with the prisoners? Let their lives be spared, in the name of humanity; but, being Indians, the stain of guiltiness requires the court gravely to consider what punishment less than death can remove it. These few, therefore, proposed that the prisoners should be sold to the West Indies.

"The court was perplexed by the difference of opinion, in a case where unanimity had been expected, and where the proper mode of procedure appeared so clear. The parts of the dilemma became more entangled with each other, the longer it was in contemplation. At length, despairing to gain a suitable decision--for the advocates of humanity, though few, were firm--they referred the decision in the boy's case to the clergymen, they being considered the ablest casuists. Doubtless the first anxiety of the reader is to know who were entrusted with so important a suit; but, when the names of Increase Mather and Dr. [John] Cotton are announced, the hopes of the Indian's friend, like the heart of Philip, breaks. [Cotton was married to Increase's sister.]

"These men proceeded at once to a thorough investigation of the subject--at least as thorough as the hunting of proofs to establish a preconceived opinion can be. Their authority was the Bible; and their selections those passages in it where the sins of parents were visited upon children, and where Philistines, Ammonites, Agagites, were hewed in pieces before the Lord-- including their children.

"From this species of evidence the decision respecting the son of a hostile Indian was short and summary. If Haman's children were executed, why should not King Philip's suffer the same fate? If Saul's house was uprooted to make room for that of David, why should not Massasoit's, branch as well as root, that the anointed of the Lord might possess the land? The voice of the ministers was therefore for death.

"Lest some may suppose that the above narrative, which ill accords with the spirit of true religion, is distorted or overcolored, we insert the answers of the two Plymouth clergymen above named to the court. The first is from Mr. Cotton.

"'The question being propounded to us by our honorable rulers, whether Philip's son be a child of death! our answer hereunto is, that we do acknowledge that rule, Deut. xxiv. 16, to be moral and therefore perpetually binding; viz. in that particular act of wickedness though capital, the crime of the parent doth not render his child a subject to the punishment by the civil magistrate; yet, upon serious consideration, we humbly conceive that the children of notorious traitors, rebels, and murderers, especially such as have been principal leaders and actors in such horrid villainies, and that against a whole nation, yea, the whole Israel of God, may be involved in the guilt of their parents, and may, *salva republica*, be adjudged to death, as to us seems evident by the scripture incidents of Saul, Achan, Haman, the children of whom were cut off by the sword of justice for the transgressions of their parents, although, concerning some of those children to be manifest, that they were not capable of being coactors therein.'

"This was signed by Samuel Arnold [the minister from Marshfield] and John Cotton, and is dated September 7, 1676. Mather holds forth in a similar strain:

"'If it had not been out of my mind when I was writing, I should have said something about Philip's son. It is necessary that some effectual course should be taken about him. He makes me think of Hadad, who was a little child when his father (the sachem of the Edomites) was killed by Joab; and, had not

132

others fled away with him, I am apt to think that David would have taken a course, that Hadad should never have proved a scourge to the next generation.'

"It is pleasing to find, amid these savage counsels, the testimony of Mr. [James] Keith, the good minister of Bridgewater. This man's opinion appears not to have been solicited; but he expresses it in a private letter; 'I long to hear what becomes of Philip's wife and son. I know there is some difficulty in that Psalm cxxxvii. 8, 9, though I think it may be considered whether there be not some specialty and something extraordinary in it. [He mentions other scripture.] I hope God will direct those whom it doth concern to a good issue.'

"Sentiments like these were echoed by those who pitied the captives; nor did it escape observation that on the side of mercy were arraigned some who had been the bravest officers of the war; and at length, in spite of the opinion of the ministers and the desires of the court, the death-sentence was not pronounced. The boy was condemned to be sold in the West Indies; and, as is usually stated, the mother shared his fate."

Actually, what happened to Wootonekanuske in the end is not known. She may have died in prison; she may have been sold into slavery along with her son, or separately from him.

Amie

Never mind that she was Massasoit's daughter, Philip's sister, Wootonekanuske's and Weetamoo's sister-in-law, and John Sassamon's mother-in-law. Amie (also known as Mionie), merits a chapter of her own, if for no other reason than the position of importance she held as the wife of Tispaquin, the powerful Black Sachem (so called because, besides being one of Philip's chief field commanders, he was also a powerful powwow, or medicine man). The lands which Tispaquin and Amie controlled included the area around Nemasket and Assawompsett (present-day Middleborough and Lakeville, Massachusetts); on many of the deeds in which, over the years, parcels of this land were sold to various English purchasers, or conveyed as gifts to other Indians, Amie's name appears along with that of her husband, evidence of the esteem in which she was held. (Descendants of Amie and Tispaquin are buried in the Royal Wampanoag Cemetery in Lakeville, Massachusetts.)

As mentioned in the previous chapter, a sister of Philip's was captured near the Taunton River, along with her uncle, Unkompoin (Akkompoin), on July 31, 1676; it is not known for certain whether it was Amie or another sister whose name has not come down to us. What became of her is not known; presumably she was sold into slavery, in the West Indies or elsewhere.

No Pew of Their Own

This chapter will, it is hoped, offer a moment of comic relief from the more serious accounts of the hardships and horrors of the war, while at the same time providing a peek at attitudes affecting women in the seventeenth century, attitudes which those of us living in the twenty-first, with its enlightened views toward the equality of the sexes, may find somewhat puzzling. The following, although it does not pertain directly to King Philip's War, tells of an incident that occurred while the war was still being fought in northern New England, and involves men who, as soldiers, had taken part in the war. It is excerpted from *The Sabbath in Puritan New England* by Alice Morse Earle.

"Perhaps no duty was more important and more difficult of satisfactory performances in the church work in early New England than 'seating the meeting-house.' Our Puritan forefathers, though bitterly denouncing all forms and ceremonies, were great respecters of persons; and in nothing was the regard for wealth and position more fully shown than in designating the seat in which each person should sit during public worship. A committee of dignified and influential men was appointed to assign irrevocably to each person his or her place, according to rank and importance.

"This seating committee sent to the church the list of all the attendants and the seats assigned to them, and when the list had been twice or thrice read to the congregation, and nailed to the meeting-house door, it became law…In all the Puritan meetings, as then and now in Quaker meetings, the men sat on one side of the meeting-house and the women on the other;

and they entered by separate doors...Of course wives had to have seats of equal importance with those of their husbands, and each widow retained the dignity apportioned to her in her husband's lifetime.

"The young men sat together in rows, and the young women in corresponding seats on the other side of the house. In 1677 the selectmen of Newbury gave permission to a few young women to build a pew in the gallery. It is impossible to understand why this should have roused the indignation of the bachelors of the town, but they were excited and angered to such a pitch that they broke a window, invaded the meeting-house, and 'broke the pue in pessis.'

"For this sacrilegious act they were fined £10 each, and sentenced to be whipped or pilloried. In consideration, however, of the fact that many of them had been brave soldiers, the punishment was omitted when they confessed and asked forgiveness. This episode is very comical; it exhibits the Puritan youth in such an ungallant and absurd light.

"In the Woburn church, the four daughters of one of the most respected families received permission to build a pew in which to sit. Here also such indignant and violent protests were made by the young men that the selectmen were obliged to revoke the permission. It would be interesting to know the bachelors' discourteous objections to young women being allowed to own a pew, but no record of their reasons is given.

"Bachelors were so restricted and governed in the colonies that perhaps they resented thought of any independence being allowed to single women. Single men could not live alone, but were forced to reside with some family to which the court assigned them, and to do in all respects just what the court ordered. Thus, in olden times, a man had to marry to obtain his freedom."

Give Us This Day
Our Daily Dread

Pardon the pun; given the piety of the Puritans, and their unshakable belief that they were God's chosen, it seems apropos for the heading of this chapter, which is all about stress.

The following incidents are examples of the stress that women settlers would have suffered on an almost daily basis, especially in the spring of 1676, when the war was going badly for the English, and no settlement outside of Boston seemed safe from Indian attack. Even the town of Plymouth, which the colonists had assumed impregnable, suffered an assault, at Clark's garrison, a scant two and one half miles from the town's center. In that attack, which occurred on March 12, eleven people, mostly women and children, were killed.

On April 21 Indians raided Scituate, a settlement in the Massachusetts Bay Colony on the South Shore, roughly halfway between Boston and Plymouth. Although in that attack the Indians were repulsed, there was no guarantee that they would not return.

As indeed they did.

On the morning of May 20, 1676, Mrs. Henry Ewell was busy in the kitchen of her home at the foot of Walnut Tree Hill, baking bread while at the same time minding her infant grandson, John Northey, who was asleep upstairs in his cradle. Ironically, we know the first name of Mrs. Ewell's husband, that of her grandson, and that of her father (he was Anthony Annable)--all males--but, as in the case of the "heroic girl at the door," not her own.

In the late seventeenth century, the baking of bread constituted one of the more difficult--and dangerous--of the culinary tasks which women were required to perform on a regular basis. As with all cooking, baking was done with open flames; fireplaces were not the cozy affairs found in today's living rooms, but were large spaces in which women stood and moved about while tending a number of separate fires. An all too common cause of fatality among women was either burning to death, from their clothing catching on fire, or succumbing to infections brought on by even minor burns incurred while handling hot implements or just moving about.

The danger of accidental death notwithstanding, the necessity to keep at least a minimal fire, a smoldering coal perhaps, going at all times, twenty-four hours a day (if a fire went out, there were no matches to simply start another), was in itself a grave responsibility. Another was ensuring that there be a continual source of yeast (organisms--fungi--that had to be kept alive, often under challenging conditions).

Mrs. Ewell probably obtained her flour from the local miller--though come to think of it, the grist mill was one of the nineteen buildings destroyed in the April raid. However she obtained it, to ready the flour for baking she first had to sift it. The night before the day of actual baking, she would have prepared a mixture of warm water, sifted flour, and yeast (from that source that she kept always on hand), leaving it by the fire to rise. In the morning she added more flour to the mixture, kneading it and fashioning it into loaves, which she then again set aside to rise.

Would she, once the loaves had risen, pop them into the oven? Well, probably not. She had to first make sure that the oven was at the right temperature--a matter, not of thermometers, but of judgment based on experience; she would thrust her hand inside and "feel" if the oven was ready for the loaves. The oven, by the way, would be built into the kitchen fireplace, at the back, without a flue; during baking its door would be left open so that smoke from it would rise up the chimney that served the fireplace as a whole. In making sure that the temperature was "just so," Mrs. Ewell could not dilly-dally. If she fiddled with the oven fire too long, the uncooked loaves which she had carefully shaped and set aside would be in danger of collapsing.

Capable housewife that she was, on the morning of May 20th Mrs. Ewell managed to coordinate dough and temperature with consummate skill. There! Though she would of course have to tend the fire from time to time, rake the coals perhaps or add fuel, to keep it at the proper level, could she now turn her attention to other pressing tasks? Alas, not so. Just as she slipped the loaves into the oven she heard war whoops. Indians were coming over the hill!

Thoroughly alarmed--she had gone through this once before--she ran toward the garrison house at Stockbridge's, forgetting in her fright her sleeping grandson. After alerting the garrison of the approach of the Indians, she suddenly remembered the forgotten child. In a panic she returned by a circuitous route to Walnut Tree Hill, where she found her home intact, the baby unawakened, and the only signs that the Indians had paid a visit, her partly baked loaves pulled from the oven.

Unfortunately the story does not end here. Mrs. Ewell snatched up little John and safely made her way back to the garrison. By the end of the day, however, the attacking Indians had burned down her house, along with those of several neighbors.

Like bread, cheese was important to the colonial diet. Moreover, cheese, if properly aged, had a much longer shelf life than baked goods; it could be prepared in the summer, then stored for consumption during the winter months and other lean times. As with bread, however, it required a great deal of labor (women's), as well as skill (also women's), to make.

It also required milk. The New England colonists had cattle, of course, but not all of these were milk-producing. To produce adequate milk for the making of cheese (as well as butter), cows needed good pasturage to begin with, and favorable weather conditions to make the grass on that pasturage grow abundantly enough for the butterfat content to be sufficiently high.

The many steps for converting fresh milk into cheese included adding rennet to the milk, then heating it until it curdled, draining off the whey, adding butter, packing the mixture into a mold, lining it with cheesecloth, and turning it in a wooden press for an hour or two to squeeze out the remaining whey--just to begin with. In the course of the next several days there would be further pressings and washings with whey and dryings, and finally storage, hopefully away from maggot-producing flies.

In *Home Life in Colonial Days*, Alice Morse Earle wrote, "Cheese was plentiful and good in all the Northern colonies. It was also an unending care from the time the milk was set over the fire to warm and then to curdle; through the breaking of the curds in cheese-basket; through shaping into cheeses and pressing in the cheese-press, placing them on the cheese-ladders, and constantly turning and rubbing them."

As with yeast, rennet (the dried inner lining of the fourth stomach of calves) had to be carefully preserved from the day of slaughter to the day, possibly months later, of cheese-making--yet another responsibility, along with maintaining a constant source of fire, not to mention live yeast, which fell to women.

Imagine the added difficulty of having to make cheese in a remote settlement during a full-scale Indian uprising. The following is taken from *Old Paths and Legends of New England* by Katherine M. Abbot.

"Among the traditions of Allen's garrison ['near Orleans Factory in Rehoboth'] is that of a woman 'turning cheese;' wishing more light, she moved back the boards of the window, and instantly, as she raised the cheese, a ball passed through it, shot by a prowling Indian."

The above incident calls to mind the story of Elizabeth Adams (born Elizabeth Paine), which adds still another tragic dimension to the plight of women in King Philip's War. She became the widow of Lieutenant Henry Adams when her husband was killed in the attack on Medfield on February 21st, 1676. After the attack she was taken to the house of the minister, where a freak accident occurred. As she slept upstairs, a gun held by Captain John Jacob in the room below accidentally discharged, killing her.

To add to the burden of women in King Philip's War, they often had to perform not only their regular household duties: cleaning house, making and mending clothes, tending to the garden, cooking, caring for small children, washing clothes, brewing beer--that was women's work, too--but also many duties usually performed by the menfolk, who might be absent because of active service in the militia, or because they had been killed or incapacitated.

And, as we have seen, if the war was hard on women settlers, it was equally hard, or harder, on Indian women. By war's end, those squaws who had not been killed or sold into slavery faced homelessness and hunger, and the harsh discrimination of the victorious English.

APPENDIX I:

Political Correctness

The following is excerpted from the preface to Ghosts from King Philip's War, *by Edward Lodi, published in 2006.*

Perhaps a brief note on language and political correctness is in order. Most Indians whom I've met--and I've met quite a few, at lectures and seminars and other events pertaining to Indian history and culture--either prefer the term "Indian" to "Native American," or have no strong feelings about the matter. It seems that it is oversensitive non-Indians who insist upon the latter term.

I am reminded of a lecture I attended a few years ago at a Reservation in Washington County, Maine, given by a member of the Passamaquoddy tribe, who was compiling a dictionary of the Passamaquoddy language. A woman in the audience, while asking a question, referred to the lecturer as a Native American. Smiling, he said: "*I'm* not a Native American; *you're* a Native American. I'm a..." and he gave the word in Passamaquoddy signifying the name for his people--which, unfortunately, I neglected to write down. The point, however, is that he was satisfied with the term Indian, which he frequently used, and so I have chosen to use it throughout this book.

In recent years the word "squaw" has been frowned upon by some, and is considered by them to be politically incorrect--to the extent that the species of duck formerly known as Oldsquaw has been renamed! However, at a lecture I attended in Connecticut (part of a week-long seminar) given by a member of the Pequot tribe on the history and culture of the Pequots and Mohegans, a member of the audience questioned the lecturer on her use of the word "squaw."

"'Squaw,'" she replied, "is an Algonquian word deriving ultimately from the word for 'blood.'" She went on to explain that "squaw" in the Algonquian language always had connotations of honor and respect. It was only in later times, as the word moved westward across the continent with European expansion, that it was used disparagingly. According to her, though there is not total agreement, most Eastern Indians consider it part of their heritage and favor its use. Following her example, I have decided to use the word "squaw" whenever appropriate.

APPENDIX II:

Fireside Industries

The following, with many omissions and some changes, is from Alice Morse Earle's Colonial Dames and Good Wives, *1895.*

"Around the great glowing fireplace in an old New England kitchen centered the homeliness and picturesqueness of an old-time home. The walls and floor were bare; the furniture was often meager, plain, and comfortless; the windows were small and ill-fitting; the whole house was draughty and cold; but in the kitchen glowed a beneficent heart that spread warmth and cheer and welcome, and beauty also when

the old rude-furnished room
burst flower-like into rosy bloom.

"The settlers built great chimneys with ample open hearths, and to those hearths the vast forests supplied plentiful fuel; but as the forests disappeared in the vicinity of the towns, the fireplaces also shrank in size. The kitchen was the housewife's domain, the chimney-seat her throne; but the furniture of that throne and the scepter were far different from the kitchen furnishings of today.

147

"We often see fireplaces with hanging cranes in pictures illustrating earliest colonial times, but the crane was unknown in those days. When the seventeenth-century chimney was built, ledges were left on either side, and on them rested the ends of a long heavy pole of green wood, called a lug-pole or back bar. The derivation of the word lug-pole is often given as meaning from lug to lug, as the chimney-side was often called the lug. Whittier wrote:

And for him who sat by the chimney lug.

"Others give it from the old English word *lug*, to carry; for it was indeed the carrying-pole. It was placed high up in the yawning chimney, with the thought and intent of its being out of reach of the devouring flames, and from it hung a motley collection of hooks of various lengths and weights, sometimes with long rods, sometimes with chains, and rejoicing in various names. Pot-hooks, pot-hangers, pot-hangles, pot-claws, pot-cleps, were one and the same; so also were trammels and crooks. Gib and gibcroke were other titles. Hake was of course the old English for hook;

On went the boilers till the hake
had much ado to bear 'em.

A twi-crook was a double hook. By these vari-named hooks were suspended at various heights over the flames pots, kettles, and other bailed cooking utensils.

"The lug-pole, though made of green wood, often became brittle or charred through too long and careless use over the hot fire, and was left in the chimney till it broke under its weighty burden of food and metal. And as within the chimney corner was a favorite seat for both old and young of the household, not only were precious cooking utensils endangered and food lost, but human life as well, as told in Judge Sewall's diary, and in other diaries and letters of the times. So, when the iron crane was hung in the fireplace, it not only added grace and convenience to the family hearth, but safety as well. On it still were hung the pot-hooks and trammels, but with shortened arms of hangers.

"The mantel was sometimes called by the old English name, clavy or clavel-piece. In one of John Wynter's letters, written in 1634, he describes his new home in Maine:

"'The chimney is large, with an oven in each end of him: he is so large that we can place our Cyttle [kettle] within the Clavell-piece. We can brew and bake and boyl our Cyttle all at once in him.'

"In olden times the pots and kettles always stood on legs, and all skillets and frying pans and saucepans stood on slender legs, that, if desired, they might be placed with their contents over small beds of coals raked to one side of the hearth. A further convenience to assist this standing over coals was a little trivet, a tripod or three-footed stand, usually but a simple skeleton frame on which the skillet could be placed. In the corner of a fireplace would be seen trivets with legs of various lengths, through which the desired amount of heat could be obtained.

"The construction of fires was no light or careless matter. Often the great backlog had to be rolled in with handspikes, sometimes drawn in by a chain and yoke of oxen. The making of the fire and its preservation from day to day were of equal importance. The covering of the brands at night was one of the domestic duties, whose non-fulfillment in those matchless days often rendered necessary a journey with fire shovel to the house of the nearest neighbor to obtain glowing coals to start again the kitchen fire.

"A domestic luxury seen in well-to-do homes was a tin kitchen, a box-like arrangement open on one side, which was set next the blaze. It stood on four legs. In it bread was baked or *roasted*. Through the kitchen passed a spit, which could be turned by an external handle; on it meat was spitted to be roasted.

149

"The brick oven was not used so frequently, usually but once a week. This was a permanent furnishing. When the great chimney was built, a solid heap of stones was placed for its foundation, and a vast and massive structure was reared upon it. On one side of the kitchen fireplace, but really a part of the chimney whole, was an oven which opened at one side into the chimney, and below an ash pit with swinging iron doors with a damper. To heat this oven a great fire of dry wood was kindled within it, and kept burning fiercely for some hours.

"Then the coal and ashes were removed, the chimney draught and damper were closed, and the food to be cooked was placed in the heated oven. Great pans of brown bread, pots of pork and beans, an Indian pudding, a dozen pies, all went into the fiery furnace together.

"To place edibles at the rear of the glowing oven, some kind of shovel must be used; and an abnormally long-handled one was universally found by the oven-side. It was called a slice or peel, or fire-peel or bread-peel. Such an emblem was it of domestic utility and unity that a peel and a strong pair of tongs were a universal and luck-bearing gift to a bride. A good iron peel and tongs cost about a dollar and a half. The name occurs constantly in old wills among kitchen properties.

"Sometimes when the oven was heated, the peel was besprinkled with meal, and great heaps of rye and Indian dough were placed thereon, and by a dexterous and indescribable twist thrown upon cabbage leaves on the oven-bottom, and thus baked in a haycock shape.

"In friendly chimney corners there stood a jovial companion of the peel and tongs, the flip-iron, or loggerhead, or flip-dog, or hottle. Flip was a drink of vast popularity, and of potent benefit in those days when fierce winters and cold houses made hot drinks more necessary to the preservation of health than nowadays. I have drunk flip, [a mixture of rum or whiskey or cider and beer and sometimes a beaten egg, into which the red-hot loggerhead has been thrust] but, like many a much-vaunted luxury of the olden time, I prefer to read of it. It is indescribably burnt and bitter in flavor.

"In nearly all old inventories a warming-pan is a part of the kitchen furnishings. A warming-pan was a shallow pan of metal, usually brass or iron, about a foot in diameter and three or four inches deep, with a pierced brass or copper cover. It was fitted with a long wooden handle. When used, it was filled with coals, and when thoroughly heated, was thrust between the icy sheets of the bed, and moved up and down to give warmth to every corner. Its fireside neighbor was the footstove, a box of perforated metal in a wooden frame, within which hot coals could be placed to warm the feet of the goodwife during a long winter's drive, or to render endurable the arctic atmosphere of the unheated churches.

"Often a lantern of pierced metal hung near the warming-pan. High up on the heavy beam over the fireplace stood usually a candlestick, an old lamp, perhaps a sausage stuffer, or a spice-mill, or a candle mold, a couple of wooden noggins, sometimes a pipe-tongs. By the side of the fireplace hung the soot-blackened, smoke-dried almanac, and near it often hung a betty-lamp, whose ill-smelling flame could supply for conning the pages a closer though scarce brighter light than the flickering hearth flame.

"By the hearth, sometimes in the chimney corner, stood the high-backed settle, a sheltered seat, while the family dye-pot often was used by the children as a chimney bench. In every thrifty New England home there stood a tub containing a pickle for salting meat. It was called a powdering-tub, or powdering trough.

"The early settlers were largely indebted to various forest trees for cheap, available, and utilizable material for the manufacture of both kitchen utensils and tableware. Wood-turning was for many years a recognized trade, dish-turner a business title. Governor Bradford found the Indians using wooden bowls, trays, and dishes, and 'Indian bowls,' made from the knots of maple trees, were much sought after by housekeepers. A fine specimen of these bowls is now in the Massachusetts Historical Society. It was originally taken from the wigwam of King Philip [see *Note* below].

"Wooden noggins (low bowls with handles) were constantly named in early inventories, and Mary Ring, of Plymouth, thought, in 1633, that a 'wodden cupp' was valuable enough to leave by will as a token of friendship. Wooden trenchers, also made by hand, were used on the table for more than a century, and were universally bequeathed by will, as by that of Miles Standish. White poplar wood made specially handsome dishes.

"Wooden pans were made in which to set milk. Wooden bread troughs were used in every home. These were oblong, trencher-shaped bowls, about a foot and a half in length, hollowed and shaped by hand from a log of wood. Across the trough ran lengthwise a stick or rod, on which the flour was sifted in a temse, or searce, or sieve. The saying, 'set the Thames on fire' is said to have been originally 'set the temse on fire,' meaning that hard labor would, by the friction of constant turning, set the wooden temse, or sieve, on fire.

"It was not necessary to apply to the wood-turner to manufacture these simply shaped dishes. Every winter the men and boys of the household manufactured every kind of domestic utensils and portions of farm implements that could be whittled or made from wood with simple tools. By the cheerful kitchen fireside much of this work was done.

"Indeed, the winter picture of the fireside should always show the figure of a whittling boy. They made butter paddles of red cherry, salt mortars, pig troughs, pokes, sled neaps, ax helves, which were sawn, whittled, and carefully scraped with glass; box traps, noggins, keelers, rundlets, flails, cheese-hoops, cheese-ladders, stanchions, handles for all kinds of farm implements, and niddy-noddys [hand reels].

"There were many domestic duties which did not waft sweet 'odors of Araby;' the annual spring manufacture of soft soap for home consumption was one of them, and also one of the most important and most trying of all the household industries.

The refuse grease from the family cooking was stowed away in tubs and barrels through the cool winter months in unsavory masses, and the wood-ashes from the great fireplaces were also thriftily stored until the carefully chosen time arrived. The day was selected with much deliberation, after close consultation with that family counselor, the almanac, for the moon must be in the right quarter, and the tide at the flood, if the soap were to 'come right.'

"Then the leach was set outside the kitchen door. Some families owned a strongly-made leach tub, some used a barrel, others cut a section from a great birch tree, and removed the bark to form a tub, which was placed loosely in a circular groove in a base made of wood or, preferably, stone. This was not set horizontally, but was slightly inclined. The tub was filled with ashes, and water was scantily poured in until the lye trickled or leached out of an inlet cut in the groove at the base. The 'first run' of lye was not strong enough to be of use, and was poured again upon the ashes.

"The wasted ashes were replenished again and again, and water poured in small quantities on them, and the lye accumulated in a receptacle placed for it. It was a universal test that when the lye was strong enough to hold up an egg, it was also strong enough to use for the soap boiling. In the largest iron pot the grease and lye were boiled together, often over a great fire built in the open air. The leached ashes were not deemed refuse and waste; they were used by the farmer as a fertilizer. Soap made in this way, while rank and strong, is so pure and clean that it seems almost like a jelly, and shows no trace of the vile grease that helped to form it.

"The dancing firelight shone out on no busier scene than on the grand candle-dipping. It had taken weeks to prepare for this domestic industry, which was the great household event of the late autumn, as soap-making was of the spring. Tallow had been carefully saved from the domestic animals killed on the farm, the honeyed store of the patient bee had been robbed of wax to furnish materials, and there was still another source of supply.

"The summer air of the coast of New England still is sweet with one of the freshest, purest plant-perfumes in the world-- the scent of bayberry. These dense woody shrubs bear profusely a tiny, spicy, wax-coated berry; and the earliest colonists quickly learned that from this plentiful berry could be obtained an inflammable wax, which would replace and supplement any lack of tallow. The name so universally applied to the plant-- candleberry--commemorates its employment for this purpose. I never pass the clumps of bayberry bushes in the early autumn without eagerly picking and crushing the perfumed leaves and berries; and the clean, fresh scent seems to awaken a dim recollection--a hereditary memory--and I see, as in a vision, the sober little children of the Puritans standing in the clear glowing sunlight, and faithfully stripping from the gnarled branches the waxy candleberries; not only affording through this occupation material assistance to the household supplies, but finding therein health, and I am sure happiness, if they loved the bayberries as I, their descendent, do.

"The method of preparing this wax was simple. The berries were boiled with hot water in a kettle, and the resolved wax skimmed off the top, refined, and permitted to harden into cakes or candles.

"When the candle-dipping began, a fierce fire was built in the fireplace, and over it was hung the largest house kettle, half filled with water and melted tallow, or wax. Candlerods were brought down from the attic, or pulled out from under the edge of beams, and placed about a foot and a half apart, reaching from chair to chair.

"Boards were placed underneath to save the spotless floor from greasy drippings. Across these rods were laid, like the rounds of a ladder, shorter sticks or reeds to which the wicks were attached at intervals of a few inches. The wicks of loosely spun cotton or tow were dipped time and time again into the melted tallow, and left to harden between each dipping. Of course, if the end of the kitchen where stood the rods and hung the wicks were very cold, the candles grew quickly, since they hardened quickly; but they were then more apt to crack.

"When they were of proper size, they were cut off, spread in a sunny place in the garret to bleach, and finally stored in candle-boxes. Sometimes the tallow was poured into molds; when, of course, comparatively few candles could be made in a day. These candles were placed in candle-sticks, or in large rooms were set in rude chandeliers of strips of metal with sockets, called candle-beams. Handsome rooms had sconces, and the kitchen often had a sliding stand by which the candle could be adjusted at a desired height.

"Snuffers were as indispensable as candlesticks, and were sometimes called snuffing-iron, or snit--from the old English verb, 'snyten,' to blow out. The snuffers lay in a little tray called a snuffer-tray, snuffer-dish, snuffer-boat, snuffer-slice, or snuffer-pan. Save-alls, a little wire frame to hold up the last burning end of candle, were another contrivance of our frugal ancestors. In no way was a thrifty housewife better known than through her abundant stock of symmetrical candles; and nowhere was a skillful and dexterous hand more needed than in shaping them.

"I am always touched, when handling the homespun linens of olden times, with a sense that the vitality and strength of those enduring women, through the many tedious and exhausting processes which they had bestowed, were woven into the warp and woof with the flax, and gave to the old webs of linen their permanence and their beautiful texture. How firm they are, and how lustrous. And how exquisitely quaint and fine are the designs. They are, indeed, a beautiful expression of old-time home and farm life."

Note: The wooden samp bowl, fashioned from the knot of an elm and allegedly belonging to King Philip, was given by Eleazer Richard to the Massachusetts Historical Society in 1804. He claimed that it had been taken by his grandfather from King Philip's wigwam when Philip was killed in 1676. The Historical Society used the bowl for casting ballots with beans and corn kernels.

APPENDIX III:

The Queen's Fort

In *The Lands of Rhode Island: As Then Were Known to Caunounicus and Miantunnoni When Roger Williams Came in 1636* (self-published in Providence in 1904), Sidney S. Rider gives a detailed description of the Queen's Fort, along with other pertinent information.

"This rude fortification stands upon a small elevation exactly on the line separating North Kingston from Exeter. It is now surrounded by timber and huge rocks. It stands upon the road running parallel with the Ten Rod road, and about one mile north from that road. The Fort is about two miles from the Wickford Junction Station on the Consolidated Railway…

"Let me enter upon some accounts of this interesting spot; interesting not alone for its historical association with the last of the Narragansetts, but also interesting because of the extraordinary character of the surface of the country. It is the extreme eastern spur of the hills which extend east and west through Exeter…The builders, taking advantage of huge boulders, laid rough stone walls between them, making a continuous line. A military friend who made [a] rough drawing says: 'There is a round bastion, or half moon, on the northeast corner of the Fort; and a Salient, or V-shaped point, or Flanker, on the west side.'

"From the south the Fort is unapproachable because of the immense mass of huge boulders with which the hill is covered; the passage by men in force among them is impossible. East, north and west the approaches are extremely difficult from the precipitous nature of the hill. The climbing of this hill is difficult even with a friend to help. What must it have been with an Indian, with his rifle in front?

"Many boulders lie within the walls of the Fort; beneath some of them are excavations sufficient to give shelter to one or two persons, but these are nothing taken in comparison with the Queen's Chamber. This extraordinary chamber is not within the Fort, but outside, west, and distant perhaps a hundred feet. It consists of an open space beneath an immense mass of boulder rocks; the tallest men can stand within it; the 'floor' is fine white sand; the entrance is so hidden that six feet away it would never be suspected; the boulders piled above it represent a thickness of fifty or sixty feet. Such is my rough description of the Queen's chamber...

"The Richard Smith house [Smith's Castle, burnt by Indians in 1676 but rebuilt shortly afterwards; restored, it is now open to the public], where the English army was in camp [in mid December, 1675], was three and three-quarters miles in a direct line, southeast from the Queen's Fort. From Smith's house to the Swamp Fort the distance in a direct line is ten miles, southwest. From the Queen's Fort to the Swamp Fort the distance in a direct line is nine miles, southwest. From the Smith house to Jireh Bull's house, on Namcook, burned by the Indians, 16th December, 1675, it was eight miles in a direct line, south.

"The question then is, where was the Indian town four miles from Smith's house where so much corn was found; and where were the Stone Walls, three and a half miles from Smith's house, from behind which the Indians fired (thirty shots) at Captain Moseley? These localities could not have been south from Smith's house, for no such town existed along that coast to Jireh Bull's house eight miles distant; it could not have been east, for Smith's house was on the shore of Narragansett Bay; it could not have been north or northeast, because the Puritan army had just marched over that country; it could not have been southwest, for the reason that from this advanced post to the Swamp Fort the distance Mr. [William] Hubbard gives [in *A Narrative of the Troubles with the Indians in New-England*, published in Boston in 1677] is fifteen or eighteen miles, whereas had it been southwest the distance would have been less than six miles; hence it must appear that the point we seek must lie either west or northwest from Smith's house. It cannot be west, for the distances render that direction impossible. It must therefore have been northwest.

"It may therefore be stated with a reasonable degree of historical accuracy that the Queen's Fort was the spot around which lay the great 'town' of the Narragansetts in 1675, and from behind the stone walls of which the Indians fired thirty shots upon the advance post of the English army on the 15th December of that year.

"The Queen was Quaiapen. She had been the wife of Mexanno, who was the eldest son of Canonicus. She was a sister to Ninigret, the Great Niantic Sachem…This Squaw-Sachem had, like all distinguished Indians, several successive names, thus, Magnus; Matantuck; the Saunck Squaw, meaning the wife of a Sachem; and the Old Queen of the Narragansetts. She was the mother of Quequaganet, the great Sachem, who sold the great tract called Pettaquamscut and other large tracts to the English. She was also the mother of Scuttape, who signed one of the Confirmation Deeds in 1659.

"She was related by blood or marriage with the most distinguished Sachems of both tribes, the Niantics and the Narragansetts. Canonicus, Mascus, Ninigret, Miantinomi, Wawaloam, the wife of Miantinomi, and the mother of Canonchet Mexanno, Quequaganet, Scuttape, all were her relations, either by blood or marriage; all were Sachems, and all being dead, Quaiapen became the great Squaw-Sachem of the Narragansetts, and her last stronghold was the Queen's Fort.

"Late in the month of June, 1676, Quaiapen with the small remnant of her tribe left living after the Swamp Fight, left the Queen's Fort on an expedition the nature of which is unknown. She had passed Nipsachook and encamped not far from Nachek on the south bank of the south branch of the Pawtuxet River, in what is now Warwick. It was a Sunday morning, July 2nd, 1676, when she was attacked by a party of Connecticut horsemen on one of their warlike excursions through Rhode Island; her band was stampeded and destroyed. It was indeed a massacre; not one escaped. Major Talcott, who commanded the troop, gives the number killed as being 238; other authorities swell the number to 300."

Recommended Reading

Flintlock and Tomahawk: New England in King Philip's War by Douglas Edward Leach (New York: The Norton Library, 1966. Copyright 1958).

Although originally published in 1958, this remains an excellent overall history of the war, especially as it occurred in southern New England.

Good Wives: Image and Reality in the Lives of Women in Northern New England 1650-1750 by Laurel Thatcher Ulrich (New York: Knopf, 1980).

Ulrich gives a detailed yet highly readable account of what the lives of women (of European descent) were like in colonial New England.

The Name of War: King Philip's War and the Origins of American Identity by Jill Lepore (New York: Alfred A. Knopf, 1998).

This is by far my favorite book about the war. Lepore, a professor of history at Harvard, analyzes the causes of the war, and its profound effect on the future course of American history. If you were to read only one other book about King Philip's War, you could not make a better choice than *The Name of War*.

Three books on the subject, all published by Rock Village Publishing and written or edited by Edward Lodi, are:

Curious Incidents in King Philip's War (2010). In addition to a number of curious incidents, the book includes a detailed time line of the war, and an extensive bibliography.

161

Ghosts from King Philip's War (2006). This is a collection of ghost stories, mysteries, and curiosities associated with the war. As with *Curious Incidents*, the emphasis is on the fascinating history behind the various tales.

The Connecticut River Valley in King Philip's War (2008). Edited by Edward Lodi, this lively narrative contains material by an earlier author, Edwin M. Bacon, as well as others.

Bibliography

Listed here are the principal sources from which material in *Women in King Philip's War* has been excerpted or referenced.

John S. C. Abbott, *History of King Philip, Sovereign Chief of the Wampanoags* (New York: Harper & Brothers, Publishers, 1899. Reprint of the 1857 edition).

Katharine M. Abbott, *Old Paths and Legends of New England* (New York: G. P. Putnam's Sons, 1904).

Pene Behrens, *Footnotes: A Biography of Penelope Pelham 1633-1703* (Montville, Maine: Spentpenny Press, 1998).

George Madison Bodge, *Soldiers in King Philip's War*, Third Edition (Boston: 1906).

Russell Bourne, *The Red King's Rebellion: Racial Politics in New England 1675-1678* (New York: Atheneum, 1990).

Thomas Church, *Entertaining Passages Relating to Philip's War* (printed by B. Green in 1716, and available in numerous reprints).

Robert Diebold, editor, *The Narrative of the Captivity and Restoration of Mrs. Mary Rowlandson* (Lancaster, Massachusetts: Lancaster Bicentennial Commission, 1975).

Samuel D. Drake, *Biography and History of the Indians of North America* (Boston: 1841).

Alice Morse Earle, *Colonial Dames and Good Wives* (Boston: Houghton, Mifflin & Company, 1895).

Alice Morse Earle, *Home Life in Colonial Days* (New York: Macmillan, 1898).

Alice Morse Earle, *The Sabbath in Puritan New England* (New York: Charles Scribner's Sons, 1893).

Other Indian Events of New England, compiled by Allan Forbes (Boston: The State Street Trust Company of Boston, 1941).

Some Indian Events of New England, compiled by Allan Forbes (Boston: The State Street Trust Company of Boston, 1934).

James Otis, *The Story of Old Falmouth* (New York: Thomas Y. Crowell & Co., 1901).

Sidney S. Rider, *The Lands of Rhode Island: As Then Were Known to Caunounicus and Miantunnoni When Roger Williams Came in 1636* (Providence: self-published, 1904).

Merril D. Smith, *Women's Roles in Seventeenth-Century America* (Westport, Connecticut: Greenwood Press, 2008).

Daniel Strock, Jr., *Pictorial History of King Philip's War* (Boston: Horace Wentworth, 1851).

Geo. J. Varney, *The Young People's History of Maine; from Its Earliest Discovery to the Final Settlement of Its Boundaries in 1842* (Portland, Me: Dresser, McLellan & Co., 1874).